A HOMESCHOOL
JOURNEY:

Life Lessons Learned along the Way

SUSA

ISBN 13: 978-1722233044
ISBN 10: 1722233044

Cover artwork by Colin Ely.

Special thanks to Kimberly Ely and Dr. Helen Wilson for their help in editing.

CONTENTS

ACKNOWLEDGMENTS

T O MY LORD and Savior, Jesus Christ. To You be all glory, honor, and praise! This book is Yours, for You downloaded it to me over the years as my patient teacher and guide. I pray that it will glorify You and encourage others to seek Your face. I love You!

Thank you to Dwight, my amazing husband, my best friend, and my partner in this wonderful journey. Thank you for loving and encouraging me and for telling me I was doing a great job, even when I did not believe it myself. Thank you for faithfully seeking God daily as you lead our family. I am honored to be your bride, and I love you with all my heart.

Thank you to Aldan, Elizabeth, and Luke, my three precious gifts from God. You are all amazing and wonderful individuals. I am incredibly blessed to be your mother and to have had the privilege of homeschooling together. Thank you for extending God's grace to me daily. I am excited to see all God has in store for you as you continue to follow Him.

Mom and Dad (Barb and Dan Lorch), thank you for raising me up in the Lord and for always loving and encouraging me.

Pastor Scott, you have impacted our family more than you will ever know, and we are eternally thankful God placed you in our lives. Your faithfulness to His Word, to prayer, and to teaching our flock is greatly appreciated.

Rodney, thank you for your friendship, your prayers, and your mentorship. You have played a vital role in the spiritual growth of our family.

The Ashton family, you are all so precious to us and we are grateful to have shared your friendship all these years.

Amy, Colette, Marla, Tracy, you are amazing women who have all inspired me to keep seeking God and growing in Him. Knowing we were in this journey together has served as great encouragement to me.

INTRODUCTION

THE BIG DAY was finally here. My three young children and I sat in the living room as I explained to them that now we were going to "have school." In anticipation of the big day, our four-year-old daughter had awakened at 6 a.m., made her bed, and dressed herself in a cute cotton dress. She was ready. After a prayer and a hearty breakfast with Dad, we headed up to our finished attic, our "schoolroom."

Truthfully, I cannot recall many other details of that first day except one. As I got out the shiny new math workbook for our five-year-old son, I opened to the first page. On the page were cute baby squirrels and acorns along with other cheerful pictures to start him on his way to learning how to count and write numbers. Our son looked at me, glanced briefly at the workbook page, then tilted his head back, rolled his eyes and exclaimed, "Oh, help me!" And so began our homeschool journey.

Homeschooling has been an exciting adventure! We have been blessed to share the majority of our days together as a family: working, playing, learning, and growing. If we could start all over again as parents, there are certainly things we would change; however, teaching our children at home is not one of them.

We have found that God has used homeschooling as a tool in our lives, a tool to reveal our strengths and weaknesses and to expose sins and character flaws that need to be changed. At times, this has been a very painful process, but it has also yielded incredible fruit and great joy. Looking back, we are thankful that God has kept us on this course. He is a patient and loving teacher.

Homeschooling is not for everyone, and it is not the only way to raise up godly children. God calls each of us to our own unique path, the one He knows is best for us. Be free to do what God is calling you to do in raising your children. As the Bible teaches us: **"For you were called to freedom, brethren; only do not turn your freedom into an opportunity for the flesh, but through love serve one another" (Galatians 5:13).**

If you have picked up this book, God has already placed homeschooling on your heart. I encourage you to pray about it with your spouse. Both of you should be in agreement before moving forward in your decision as to how to train up your children.

My prayer is that the words I write will serve to encourage and refresh you. I pray that you will find the encouragement to begin homeschooling your children, or that you will be renewed in your resolve to continue homeschooling them. God has a plan to teach you and to mold you while you guide and instruct your children. God created families. It is His will for you to raise your children to love and serve Him. If He has called you, He will empower you. Amen!

CHAPTER 1

Why Homeschool?

WHY DID YOU choose to homeschool your children? This is an excellent question and one that my husband and I received often. It is one we would answer slightly differently now than when we first began our homeschool journey. Back when we started homeschooling, we would have said we wanted to be the ones to impact our children, to teach them about God and the Bible, to spend more time with them, shaping them into the people God wanted them to become. It felt like a simple response. Now nearly twenty years and three graduates later, we would add many more details to our original, simple beginning. Isn't that just how God works? He starts us off small, showing us the next step to take; then, little by little, He leads us deeper. When we look back, we are amazed at how far we have come. He is a good and patient teacher.

Now that our homeschooling has come to an end, we can look back at the lessons we have learned and the benefits we have reaped because of our choice to follow God's prompting. We have seen first-hand how homeschooling has advantages spiritually, emotionally, socially, mentally, and physically. So, if we were to expand upon reasons why homeschooling is an incredibly blessed choice, this is what we would say:

Biblical Reasons to Homeschool

God's Word provides us with instructions for parenting. It says, **"Train up a child in the way he should go, even when he is old he will not** depart from it" **(Proverbs 22:6).** God wants us to guide our children in His ways and teach them to trust and obey Him. The Bible says, **"That the generation to come might know, even the children yet to be born, that they may arise and tell them to their children, that they should put their confidence in God and not forget the works of God, but keep His commandments" (Psalms 78: 6,7).**

God clearly tells parents that it is their job to train their children in His ways. It is not the job of the church, the Sunday school teacher, the youth pastor, or the public or private school teacher. Parents are to train their children. The responsibility falls on them and they are accountable to God for the job that they do. The Bible says, **"You shall therefore impress these words of mine on your heart and on your soul; and you shall bind them as a sign on your hand, and they shall be as frontals on your forehead. You shall teach them to your sons, talking of them when you sit in your house and when you walk along the road and when you lie down and when you rise up. You shall write them on the doorposts of your house and on your gates..." (Deuteronomy 11: 18-20).**

Do you see when and where we are to train our children? When we sit, walk, lie down, and rise up. Clearly, training our children is a full-time job, all day, every day. We are to model God's love for our children, and we are to train them in His Word so that they would know, love, and obey God on their own.

Homeschooling your children provides you with the most time possible to instruct them and train them up in the Lord. Let me share some of the blessings and advantages of homeschooling your children as you raise them.

Spiritual Training

When you homeschool your children, you can take the time to make Bible reading the priority of the day. We used to read a chapter or two of the Bible, discuss it, share prayer requests, pray, then recite scripture aloud together. When the kids were small we used a felt board to give them a visual to go with the Bible story or lesson. Bible verses were copied for handwriting practice, and God-honoring curriculum was carefully selected.

Having your kids at home affords them opportunities to see how you handle yourself there as well as on the phone, on errands, during "interruptions" in your day, and in all of life. It is a big responsibility as they watch you as their real-life model Christian! None of us do it perfectly, but wouldn't you rather be the example your children follow than teachers and students over whom you have little or no control?

Homeschooling allowed us time to take a family mission trip to Nicaragua. What a wonderful opportunity to serve others while also realizing how blessed we are to live as we do! Your children can serve along with you at church, in the nursery, in a nursing home, in your community, on mission trips, and more. The possibilities are endless.

In this way, all of life becomes a lesson. For example, when our older son was small, he saw a sunset and exclaimed, "God made that!" This same son purposed to share the gospel with a friend from his soccer team at a bonfire we held at our farm. After the event, he joyfully shared with us how he had talked with his friend and then prayed with him to accept the Lord as his Savior. He was trained to know that God is a part of everything and He is the most important part of our lives. He witnessed the adults in his life praying with and for others and their needs, and for their salvation. The Holy Spirit became alive and active in him, which helped him to share his faith with another.

A different time, my husband and younger son went to check on our beehives. My husband told our young son to wait down the hill a short distance from the hive to prevent him from being stung. As my husband checked on the bees, they became agitated and were flying everywhere. When he looked up, he was surprised to see our son standing nearby so that he could see what was going on. Bees swarmed all around him. When my husband expressed his concern, our young son replied, "It's okay, Daddy, I prayed!" Already, at his young age, our son had learned that God can be trusted to hear and answer our prayers.

In another instance, our daughter had wanted a pony in the worst way. She had her own little business where she raised chickens and sold the eggs in our store, and she began saving her money from the sale of her eggs so that she could eventually buy a pony for herself. One day at church, she felt compelled to donate all of her birthday money to the victims of a recent tsunami, which had occurred halfway around the world. Sometime later, a local veterinarian called us and asked us if we wanted a pony. Someone wanted to get rid of it and give it to a good home. God is so good! Our daughter learned that God always provides for us, and He loves to give us good gifts.

A different time, our young son decided that he wanted to tithe. He brought his money to church and put it in the offering plate. After church, his friend handed him a container of turtle food as a present, not knowing that our son's beloved pet turtle had recently died. As he stood holding the food, a church member spotted it and asked if he had a turtle. Our son explained that he had owned a turtle but it had recently died. The lady asked him if he would like to have her daughter's turtle. Her daughter was in college and no longer interested in caring for her pet. The lady offered our son a turtle, tank, filter, and food. All this occurred before we even left church! Isn't God amazing?!

Now, would these responses have taken place if our children were not homeschooled? Yes, perhaps. But, I strongly believe that they happened because of the time they were nurtured and taught at home. When you don't have to rush your children off to the bus in the morning, or push them to complete homework at night, you have much more time to spend on the details required in training them and growing them up in the Lord. God is a part of everything and you can make your children aware of His presence throughout your days. As you learn and grow in the Lord, your children do, too.

Emotional/Character Training

One great benefit of homeschooling is that your children can grow up nurtured in an emotionally safe, accepting, and loving environment. Children raised in a secure and loving atmosphere, without fear of ridicule by outsiders, have a huge emotional advantage in life. Let's face it, no matter how excellent a teacher is, nobody will love your children more than you do!

Time to work on relationships is another huge blessing. When your children argue or act in a less than ideal way, you can set aside your schoolwork to deal with the problem at hand. Because you have your children home all day, character issues will readily appear, and you can prayerfully take the time to handle them in the best possible way. I found Pam Forster's *For Instruction in Righteousness* to be a wonderful guide. As I like to say, it is a reference book with all of your sins in black and white. Basically, it has an index of sinful root behaviors and Bible passages that can help you deal with those issues. The book also provides some positive reinforcement ideas as well as some negative consequences that can be used in training your children. Perhaps you will want to read a book on love languages or on peacemaking with your children to help them learn to get along better with their siblings and others. You have the freedom and flexibility to follow the Holy Spirit's leading as you train your children.

Obedience and attitudes of the heart can be addressed. Sometimes, negative attitudes and behaviors are subtler, like procrastinating or acting in a passive but rebellious manner. When you are not rushing to leave the house for the day, you can take time to notice and address these less obvious character issues. You can see the strengths in your children and affirm them just as you can pray through and work on their weaknesses.

Homeschooling allows ample opportunity to practice good time management techniques. In our family, we ate breakfast, then read the Bible, completed schoolwork, worked on chores, then had free time. When our children were small, I directed the use of their time. We explored the subjects I chose and completed our tasks in the order I chose them. As our children matured, I gave them each a planner. After we completed our Bible studies, science, and history together, our children had a choice in the order they completed their reading, writing, language, math, and other work. As they completed assignments, they marked them off in their planners. Chores were posted daily on a list on the refrigerator. When schoolwork was complete, our children would check the chore list and complete their chores, marking them off when finished. After all schoolwork and chores were done, the children had free time to use as they desired. Free time was a big motivator to complete all work in a timely manner.

During the school day, we also allowed some time for snacks or breaks. Sometimes, if the kids seemed "itchy" we would send them out to do a few chores first to expend some extra energy and make it easier to focus on schoolwork. Of course, constant monitoring was required. We had to follow up and make sure the schoolwork and the chores were complete and done with excellence. Plenty of times, we had to call a child back from play because chores or schoolwork were not completed or done well. Training is a process that requires a lot of time and focused energy.

By making mistakes as young children, our kids learned to manage time. I remember quite a few days in which one of the children was in tears because he was the last one done after taking one too many Lego breaks! Children learn by making mistakes along the way. All of the hard work paid off and our children eventually learned to manage their own time well.

Homeschooling allows time and opportunity for you to instill a strong work ethic in your children. There are ample jobs around any home: mowing the yard, weeding, simple repairs, cleaning, laundry, meal preparation, and more. Our children had household and farm chores to do simply because they belonged to our family; further, we chose not to give an allowance for completing chores. If our children wanted to earn money, all they had to do was to ask and we provided them with "paying jobs" around the farm and in our butcher shop. When our oldest son wanted to purchase a 4-wheeler at the age of 12, my husband offered him a certain dollar amount for every deer he skinned for our business during hunting season. That diligent young man woke up early and headed to work, completed his schoolwork, went to wrestling practice, ate dinner, then hustled back to work for a couple of hours before bedtime. That year he skinned 1,000 deer and bought himself a new 4-wheeler. He put the vehicle away, changed the oil, and took excellent care of his purchase; he knew the hard work that went into buying it, and he was invested. What a wonderful life lesson that was for him on so many levels. Each of our children purchased their own vehicles for cash, usually in advance of earning their driver's license.

They have maintained their own bank accounts and have learned how to work hard for the things they desire.

If you don't have a farm or business, your children can begin apprenticeships or jobs when they are old enough. Because of flexibility in your school schedule, your children may have many more work opportunities available. We have hired many homeschooled students because they were free during the work day. Perhaps a neighbor needs some help with yardwork or painting. Pray about it, and God will show you the opportunities before you.

Homeschooling is not just for the kids! As you learn and grow along with your kids, God will stretch you and sharpen you into maturity in Christ. Impatience, irritability, selfishness, and other sinful attitudes and behaviors often come to light in us as well as in our children when we are together all day every day.

Early on in our homeschool years, I was having a particularly difficult season. I was impatient and frustrated and so were my kids. I began to think they would be better off in a public school with a more patient teacher. A homeschool magazine sample appeared one day in my mailbox. I did not subscribe to the magazine and have only received a few issues in the 17 years we homeschooled; however, God had that one in my mailbox for a reason. When I opened it up, there was an article about why most people quit homeschooling. One of the primary reasons mentioned was parent-child conflict. The article claimed that parents who stopped homeschooling and enrolled their children in school often found a reduction in conflicts with their children. However, the author pointed out that the conflicts were absent mainly because the children were away most of the day. The author went on to suggest that the character flaws and sinful attitudes and behaviors were still present in us and in our children, yet they were no longer confronted but merely swept under the rug.

I knew in that moment God was speaking to me and encouraging me not to give up; the work was hard, but the rewards were greater. Homeschooling is a full-time job and the dividends are enormous!

Social Development

What about socialization?? Any parent who has ever homeschooled will tell you that this is perhaps the most frequently asked question. People who have grown up attending school from ages 5-18, eight hours a day, 180 days per year, cannot fathom that children can be socialized any other way. Consider for a moment your own insecurities or feelings of self-doubt. Do any of them stem back to your childhood school experiences? Many people would say that they do. Fear of looking stupid, fear of the teacher or other students, performance anxiety, and numerous other "hang-ups" can usually be traced back to their early days in school. School, by its very nature, is an artificial environment. When, in your lifetime, will you ever again be contained in a room with thirty peers of the exact same age and required to complete assigned activities in a designated manner and time frame? If your first-grade child is in a room all day with thirty other seven-year-olds and only one adult, do you think he will pick up all of the good habits of the immature children around him, or will he learn the bad ones?

Homeschooling provides an atmosphere where children are surrounded by people of many different ages. A child will interact with parents, siblings, neighbors, store clerks, the postman, and numerous people in all walks of life as he lives life within the security of his family. Homeschooled children generally interact more frequently with adults and have less time with peers. Because this time with peers is limited, parents can work through any issues that arise and can offer godly counsel and a biblical perspective. I will never forget the day I was driving our junior-high-aged son to football practice at the public school. As he shared with me the attitude and language of some of the kids, he commented that he would be a different person if he were there all day every day, and he thanked me for homeschooling him.

Young children have siblings to play with and do not need many other friendships. As children grow, the need for interaction can be met in a variety of ways. Homeschooled children participate in community and school sports, family gatherings, 4-H clubs, community activities, church events and organizations, music lessons, drama groups, mission trips, and a host of other activities. Families can serve others together in nursing homes, churches, community events, and on mission trips.

We have had like-minded homeschool families whose children have grown up alongside ours. These family friendships are precious and have given our children wonderful conversations, traditions, and stability. We have taken field trips and overnight trips together and have spent many holidays together creating lifetime memories. My children feel as if they have a second home in the presence of these dear friends.

We have observed that homeschooled children are generally happy to meet and play with children of any age. They are thankful to interact with other children and adults regardless of age. Children gain leadership skills and confidence as they learn to engage with people in all stages of life. Both of our sons were chosen by their teammates to serve as captains of their varsity wrestling teams. The students and coaches all recognized their integrity, hard work, and leadership skills. Socialization?? A great reason to keep your children at home!

Academics and Life Skills

One of the primary academic advantages to homeschooling is the utilization of one-on-one instruction or tutoring. Homeschooling allows for more individualized instruction, which permits you to provide each child with a personalized, customized education. How could anything be better? Curriculum can be carefully chosen to reflect your values. We used science materials that supported the creationist view rather than the evolutionist view found in the majority of textbooks. The Apologia publishing company has a host of wonderful science materials which use the Bible as a foundation and are very thorough in their coverage. This is helpful in preparing students for college, if desired. For history, we read many biographies aloud to our children and discussed them or completed fun projects, which allowed for a greater recall. Sometimes we allowed the interests of our children to dictate a particular study topic. When our daughter was in late elementary school, she studied the history of the horse and most of her reading, writing, history, and science centered around that topic. Another year, we studied the history of science all together, reading biographies of famous scientists and performing experiments which illustrated their original findings.

As a parent, you are free to be as creative or as structured as you desire. Each year can be different. One year you can do unit studies; another year you can use a literature-based approach or use more structured materials. The possibilities are endless. Each year, I prayed about what the Lord would have us study the next year. Then, I would plan, order the necessary materials, and step out in faith, trusting that God would continue to guide us. Occasionally, mid-year, I might abandon certain materials or purchase different books as God redirected. Most of the time, we continued on the planned course for that particular year. Did everything go perfectly smoothly? Were our days full of perfect joy and learning? Of course not! Homeschooling is hard work and can at times be tedious and frustrating. But I would not have traded it for anything! Day after day, we were together as a family.

Another huge benefit of choosing your own curriculum is that you can accommodate each child's unique learning style. If you are unfamiliar with learning styles, I recommend that you purchase a book on the topic to learn about the best ways to reach each of your children. Basically, there are four main ways people take in and process information and these learning styles are generally called: visual, tactile or kinesthetic, reading/writing, and auditory. Most people benefit by instruction presented in all styles, but many learners gravitate toward a dominant learning modality.

One of our sons is a strong auditory learner. He did not need to see pictures when I read a story aloud, and he could listen to the most monotone reader recite a story. Whatever he heard, he remembered. Hearing a word and recording the letters to spell out each sound was far easier for him than looking at a word and decoding it. Consequently, he was a late reader, catching on almost overnight at the age of eight. What a blessing that he was not in a public-school setting in which, at the age of six (the designated "proper time" to learn to read) he would most likely have been labeled as having a "learning disability." By the fifth grade, this same son tested above the 90th percentile in standardized reading tests. Thomas Edison was older than eight when he learned to read, after having been thrown out of school and declared too dumb to learn. I wonder if he was an auditory learner as well!

You can try a variety of techniques, games, and materials to keep you and your children interested and learning, and you can adjust your pace as well. When our children needed to learn their multiplication tables, I held up flashcards while they bounced up and down on Hoppity-hops. At one point in our learning, we stopped working in our math books for several weeks to spend time memorizing math facts. Pacing is entirely up to you. When your children know a topic, you can skip it or move on. You are also free to move more slowly if needed.

Real life learning opportunities are among the biggest advantages of homeschooling. You can take time to teach your children how to write checks and manage money. My kids loved sitting down with me at my desk and writing checks to pay real bills. They nervously held their pens as they carefully filled out each check and corresponding envelope as I sat beside them. How important they felt that they were doing something with real-life implications! Also, they learned how much the phone, internet, and electricity cost!

Our children answered phones and took holiday meat orders from the time they were around ten years old. We occasionally gave them math learning activities to complete as we grocery shopped. They utilized their knowledge of unit conversions to figure out how many seeds were needed to plant our corn and bean crops. They were present for family discussions about household and business purchases. Meal planning and preparation, home and car repairs, farm work: these real-life activities could be learned together at home.

While your children are young, they can learn so many skills at home as they do them with you. It will take you longer to finish the job if you include them, but down the road you will have wonderfully capable helpers! When your kids are older, they can job shadow or engage in apprenticeships; there are numerous possibilities and opportunities for real-life learning.

Co-ops and field trips are wonderful opportunities to add some fresh sparks to your learning as well. Co-ops can be formal or informal, with many families or just a few. During our early homeschool years, we participated in a couple of low-key informal co-ops. This allowed us to have more flexibility in our schedule to accommodate the demands of our farm and business. We also planned a field trip with one other family each month. We went to the bakery, the firehouse, museums, and historical sites. Sometimes we even traveled by train, another exciting part of the adventure. Our children still remember these trips with great fondness. Our family trips around the US and overseas also added a great deal to the life experiences of our children.

A huge benefit of homeschooling is the flexibility it allows within your family schedule. If a friend or family member is sick or in need of help, you can take the time and make a meal, do yardwork, or offer support. Schoolwork can be shifted to a later time or a later date if needed. When our children were young, our school week ran from Tuesday through Saturday. Because our store is open Saturdays, we have to work, and our weekends consist of Sundays and Mondays. This schedule allowed us Sundays and Mondays as family days. When our children reached junior high school age and wanted to participate in public school sports, we shifted our schedule back to the usual Monday through Friday school week. If our cows escaped the fence, or if my husband needed help with a farm project, we were available. Our children often visited their grandparents and frequently had lunch with their widowed grandmother or helped her with household projects. Because we could manage our time as desired, we fit school around life rather than become slaves to a rigid schedule.

Monitoring the use of electronics, media, and cell phones is another important benefit to having your children home with you. You can keep your computer in a visible spot and monitor its use. Likewise, you can set limits for computer and TV time, as well as for cell phone use. **Psalms 101:3** states, **"I will set no worthless thing before my eyes,"** and that is the standard to keep in mind.

Our children were in junior high before smartphones became popular, so it was a bit easier for us to monitor their use than it is for today's new parents. We did not permit them during school time or during meals, and the phone needed to be left downstairs each night; we did not permit our children to keep them in their rooms. Our computer was kept in the living room in a prominent location, and our TV was stored behind closed cabinet doors until we decided to watch something as a family.

As parents, you will need to model good behavior when it comes to media. Many parents check out of the home via social media (Facebook, surfing the internet, texting, etc.), and it is important to be "present" when you homeschool your children. As you seek the Lord about this and other aspects of your parenting, God will certainly guide you.

When you homeschool your children through their high school years, you have the incredible opportunity to customize their education for their goals and callings. There is no need for a generic, one-size-fits-all education. As you teach your children to seek the Lord and follow His leading, you can help guide them in the way in which they should go (see **Proverbs 22:6**). You can utilize on-line and community college classes, traditional materials and textbooks, apprenticeships and work experiences, tutors, and any other means to best train up your children.

Our older son studied meat science and accounting to prepare him to work in our business. He worked in our shop in an apprenticeship and took some business classes at the community college. He read Christian books about dating and seeking God's best for his future wife. Our daughter studied home economics and read books to help her become a godly wife and mother, and she completed anatomy and chemistry classes to prepare her for nursing school. Our youngest took classes at the community college that would help prepare him for business studies at a four-year university. We always tried to seek God's leading, while making sure we left as many doors open as possible. All three of our children completed two years of a language and the necessary math, science, and English classes so that, if needed, they would be equipped for college.

Physical Development and Health

You can provide a safe atmosphere for your children where they can remain physically active and develop healthy lifestyle habits. Homeschooling can provide a safe atmosphere, free of drugs, violence, and bullying. Of course, siblings can argue and fight, but it is much easier for you to monitor and instruct your children at home than it is for a teacher with thirty students. Also, if your child is sick or injured, you can adjust your instructional time accordingly. For example, our older son often struggled with asthma. Because he was home, we could treat his asthma and monitor his health while including him in educational activities. Likewise, when our youngest broke his leg, he could still complete schoolwork along with his siblings.

Homeschool students are not required to sit at a desk the majority of the day, so they can automatically be more active. They can read on the couch or outside in a hammock; they can take nature walks, bike rides, and field trips. Chores can be completed throughout the day to allow for movement and a break in the routine. Because children can complete schoolwork earlier in the day, they can be free to play on public school or community sports teams. They can complete projects or play games. In short, homeschool students have more freedom to move and be active during the entire day.

In addition to opportunities for exercise, homeschool students can learn about good nutrition and take an active role in food planning and preparation. You can teach your children how to select a nutritious menu and then take them with you to the grocery store to purchase healthy ingredients. Then, you can work together to prepare wholesome meals for your family. By working alongside you over the course of many years, your children will naturally learn many aspects of nutrition and food preparation. Your influence can help them develop good eating habits to last a lifetime.

Some Challenges and Rewards

While homeschooling has numerous benefits spiritually, emotionally, socially, cognitively, and physically; it is not without challenges. One of the most obvious is the lack of time the parent has for outside activities. Often, women's Bible studies, time with friends, hobbies, shopping, coffee out, and other social activities need to be sacrificed so that you can spend time focusing on child training and family relationships.

The good news is that most sacrifices you make now yield rewards later. I can honestly say that I never regret even one minute of the time

I have been blessed to spend with my children. Your children will grow up and you will once again have time for more outside activities. However, you will have the reward of strong family connections and the knowledge that you did your utmost to train your children in the Lord. If you take the school calendar of 180 days per year, and multiply that by 7 hours per day times 13 years, you have 16,380 *more* hours with your children than parents who send their kids away to school. If you figure that you have 16 waking hours per day and divide 16,380 by 16, you end up with over 1,000 more days with your kids; that's nearly 3 years of waking hours! This does not even account for bus rides or homework time.

With all of this time, sins and character flaws are exposed. Working through conflicts and relational issues can be the most exhausting part of homeschooling; however, the pay-offs here are enormous. As you grow in your faith and mature in your Christian walk, your children will learn alongside you.

In addition to the investment of time in homeschooling, there is also a financial cost. Books and materials, field trips, and music lessons all cost money. Also, one parent must be home, which may mean living on one income. The flip side is, you can utilize the library and many free materials found on the internet. There are also plenty of web locations where homeschool parents sell used curricula.

There will be academic gaps. No two parents are perfectly skilled in or excited about every academic discipline. Let's face it: we are going to do a better job teaching what we know and love best. But, the same is true in public or private school. Each teacher comes with his own personal bias and skill set. While you may worry that your own weaknesses will hold your children back, you can rest in the fact that there will always be gaps and that is where we can trust the Lord to fill in those missing pieces as He sees fit.

Finally, homeschooling is a lot of work. It is not for the fainthearted or lazy. There is planning, purchasing, grading and monitoring, meals, laundry, and extra messes from being home all day. There is no doubt this is a full-time job! But you get to decide how to spend time and resources; you get to spiritually guide your children and instill strong character traits within them; you get to teach them the values and life skills you deem most important. Anything of value requires hard work, and homeschooling is no exception. The rewards are worth the cost!

Homeschooling provides an exceptional atmosphere for guiding children into the people God has created them to be. In choosing how to spend our days, we tried to keep this question as our compass: When our children leave home, what do we desire for them? For us, some of the most important goals were:

- Salvation: We desired that each child had his own relationship with Jesus Christ as Lord and Savior and was committed to continue to love, seek, and serve God all his days.
- How to Learn: We aimed to have our children know "how to learn" so throughout life they would keep learning and growing and adapting as needed.
- The ability to function well in life.
- Proficiency in reading, writing, and communicating.
- A strong work ethic, and a desire to serve others.
- Good relationships with parents, siblings, and others.

Keeping end goals in mind will help you establish a framework for instructing your children in the way they should go. Spiritually, emotionally, socially, mentally, physically: homeschooling has so many advantages. If God is calling you to homeschool your children, step out in faith! He will help you and provide what you need to stay the course. Don't miss out on the blessing!

CHAPTER 2

It's All About Relationships

HOMESCHOOLING HAS BECOME increasingly popular over the past two decades, and if you ask parents why they choose to homeschool their children you will obtain a variety of answers. Better academic opportunities, freedom to choose what, when, and how our children learn, flexibility for travel or field trips, religious instruction, impartation of values, and avoidance of negative peer influences are among the reasons cited by many for homeschooling. While I agree with the validity and value of these reasons and while my husband and I embraced many of them in our initial decision to homeschool, I have grown to realize and appreciate a more all-encompassing reason to homeschool our children: relationships.

First and foremost, as parents, we need to have a right and ever deepening relationship with God. As we grow in our faith and teach our children about God and His ways, we will become more effective disciples for the kingdom and more effective as parents. Secondly, we need to focus on our marriage relationship and keep it as a priority. Finally, we need to focus on our relationship with our children by teaching them to be rightly related to God, to parents, to siblings, and to others.

First things First: Our Relationship with God

As homeschool moms, we have hundreds of tasks that call out for our time and attention throughout the day. This struggle seems to be universal. Think back to the days before you were a wife and a mother;

when and how did you spend your time? Think ahead to when your children are grown; where will your focus be? Now back to the present; how are you to choose the best above all that is good? I believe the answer to each of these questions can be found in keeping our priorities as God designed them to be.

In *My Utmost for His Highest*, Oswald Chambers shares his insight on this topic:

> We do not know what God is after, but we have to maintain our relationship with Him whatever happens. We must never allow anything to injure our relationship with God. The main thing about Christianity is not the work we do, but the relationship we maintain and the atmosphere produced by that relationship. That is all God asks us to look after, and it is the one thing that is being continually assailed. (159)

When Jesus was asked what the greatest commandment is, He replied, **"'You shall love the Lord your God with all your heart, and with all your soul, and with all your mind.' This is the great and foremost commandment. The second is like it, 'You shall love your neighbor as yourself.' On these two commandments depend the whole Law and the Prophets" (Matthew 22: 37-40).**

Clearly, God is to be our highest priority. We are to love Him with our *heart*, our *soul*, and our *mind*. From our heart comes our affection, fondness, feeling, attachment, respect, and tenderness. God wants to be our first love. Remember when you first fell in love with your husband and all of those feelings of love, affection, and tenderness were at the forefront of everything you said and did? God wants our heart. God also wants our soul, our deep innermost part, that which makes us who we are. He created us and loves us more than any human ever could, and He wants us to love Him back with our deepest selves. Finally, God wants us to love Him with our minds. We do have a choice in what we think about. Thousands of thoughts pop into our heads daily, and it is up to us to decide upon which of these thoughts we will dwell. God wants us to choose to love Him in our thoughts.

When we spend time with God and keep Him as our priority, the other pieces of our life, including our homeschooling, will fall together. We are promised in God's Word: **"But seek first His kingdom and His righteousness, and all these things will be added to you"** (Matthew 6:33).

Taking Thoughts Captive

As I move through this journey of life, I realize more and more the power that my thoughts have to sway the course of my moments, my days, and my life. The way that I choose to think about a person or situation can alter my whole outlook and mood. This has been a lesson I have been learning throughout our homeschool journey; however, it is one that continually surfaces as a lesson I have not mastered.

For example, one morning when I woke up, I reflected on a wedding my family had attended. A deep sadness engulfed me, and I had to get up, read God's Word, then take a run as I asked God to give me His thoughts. I was thinking that my best years were behind me, my kids would soon be grown and on their own. What, then, was my purpose? I wished I could go back and re-live the years when we were newly married and life, with all of its possibilities and dreams, stretched before me. These thoughts were not the thoughts God desires me to have. As the Bible says, **"Do not say, 'Why is it that the former days were better than these?' For it is not from wisdom that you ask about this"** (Ecclesiastes 7: 10).

Looking back at the past and thinking those years were somehow better than the present is not wise. I need to learn from the past, be thankful in the present, and hope for the wonderful future God has in store for me. I believe that the enemy wants to keep us in regret over what has passed, or in worry over the future so that we miss the present. With God's help, I am choosing thanksgiving and endeavoring to follow His command: **"Rejoice always; pray without ceasing; in**

everything give thanks; for this is God's will for you in Christ Jesus" (I Thessalonians 5:16-18).

As I reflect on my thoughts of past years, I remember wonderful times; however, I also remember sad and difficult ones. When my kids were very small and we attended a picnic, I had to run after them the whole time and had no time to visit other adults. I remember thinking that I would never get to sit down and visit again at a picnic. This was ridiculous thinking, I know. But these were my thoughts nonetheless. Now, I sometimes think how I wish I had a little one to chase, to read to, and to snuggle with, for the years passed too quickly. Along the way, I have thought many "if only's."

If only I did not have to do the business paperwork, I could really focus completely on homeschooling and the kids; if only I were more confident I would be more joyful; if only my kids enjoyed academics more we could have more fun; if only I were a stronger person I would be a better wife and helper to my husband; if only I had been less critical over the years the people around me would have benefited; if only I could go back and re-do the last ten years I would never get angry, and I would be a better mother and wife; if only I had been a better mother my kids would be kinder to one another; if only we had more children; if only I were different; if only my husband were different; if only I were more like so-and-so or had a life like hers...

These thoughts are rarely productive and they often cause despair and heartache rather than hope or resolve to change. I have realized that every moment I waste on these negative thoughts steals a part of my life. The enemy loves us to get off-track with our thinking, for it paralyzes us for today and makes us ineffective servants of our King. My heart aches at how often I have meditated on negative thoughts rather than working on taking them captive and allowing God's thoughts to replace my own.

I am so thankful that God is a restorer and a redeemer. He can take what has been devoured or lost and make our lives better than we imagined. As the Bible says, **"Then I will make up to you for the years that the swarming locust has eaten" (Joel 2:25).** I do not need to live in regret, but I can rejoice, knowing that God will restore anything I have lost. Additionally, He always has good plans ahead for each of us. As He says in His Word, **"'For I know the plans that I have for you,'** declares the Lord, 'plans for welfare and not for calamity to give you a future and a hope'" (Jeremiah 29:11). What a glorious promise that is!

God's Word reveals that our thoughts are a choice. **2 Corinthians 10: 5** states, "**We are destroying speculations and every lofty thing raised up against the knowledge of God, and we are taking every thought captive to the obedience of Christ.**" What we choose to think on can change the course of our lives. When I think of the word "captive," I imagine a prisoner or a wild animal held against his will in a secure area where he cannot escape and where he cannot harm others. Webster defines *captive* as: "One, as a prisoner, who is forcibly confined, restrained, or subjugated. Held as a prisoner. Under restraint or control" (Websters II New Riverside University Dictionary).

Just as captives have the possibility and the desire to escape, so do these negative thoughts, for they are of the enemy and he seeks to destroy our lives and our impact for God's kingdom. We are called to keep our thoughts under restraint so they cannot harm us or others. How are we to do this? What are we to think on? The Bible gives us guidance for our thoughts: "**Finally, brethren, whatever is true, whatever is honorable, whatever is right, whatever is pure, whatever is lovely, whatever is of good repute, if there is any excellence and if anything worthy of praise, dwell on these things**" (Philippians 4:8). Thus, we are to think, or dwell on, thoughts that are positive and uplifting.

Taking our thoughts captive is an ongoing process throughout life. Little by little, as we practice replacing negative thought patterns with the truths God reveals to us in His Word, we will be transformed. If we continue to ask God for help, He promises to hear and answer our prayers.

When our youngest son left home for his first year of college, he struggled to be joyful and thankful and instead wished he could be back home where it was comfortable. He progressed through the normal range of emotions that many freshmen experience as they make the transition to life away from home for the first time. As I prayed for him and encouraged him, I felt led to send him this letter. It reflected what God was teaching me about my thoughts and what I, in turn, hoped my son would learn at a much younger age, so that he could have a lifetime of God's joy. I have copied the letter for you here:

"Through Him then, let us continually offer up a sacrifice of praise to God, that is, the fruit of lips that give thanks to His name. And do not neglect doing good and sharing, for with such sacrifices God is pleased" (Hebrews 13:15, 16).

Luke, I read these verses during my quiet time today and feel challenged to truly learn to continually give praise and be thankful.

Lord, this problem seems hard, but thank you that you are helping me and working on my behalf. You give me wisdom.

Thank you, Lord, for the blessing of being able to work hard. You give me strength even though it is hard.

Thank you, Lord, for providing all my needs, for loving me, for blessing me with a wonderful family.

Thank you, Lord, for breakfast.

The sunrise is beautiful; I praise your name!

I am tired, Lord, and overwhelmed. Thank you that you will give me the rest and wisdom I need. Thanks for guiding my path.

I am also challenged to do good and share, for it pleases God. Sometimes I get so focused on my own "to do" list that I forget to look around me and really see people. There are so many ways I can bless others that cross my path, and I pray God makes me more aware. A smile, a conversation, an offer to help or to pray, giving my time or spending some money for someone in order to bless them. I need to do more of this now and pray God will help me.

When I was in college there were so many needy people around me. I wish I had known these truths then and had reached out more in love. I could have impacted more lives for God's kingdom.

You have such wisdom, Luke. When I see you, and how you interact with others, I am so proud of you and so honored to be your mom. From the time you were a small boy you could see people's hurting hearts. God has given you compassion and mercy and you ARE impacting the world for Him!

I encourage you to practice giving thanks in all things. God is growing you and you are becoming more like Him. He has an awesome life for you-incredible surprises and blessings all along the way. Don't forget to see those around you and reach out to "do good" and "share." In blessing others, you will be blessed!

I am working on this too and appreciate your prayers. I love you so very much! You are an incredible and amazing gift from God and I thank Him daily for all things concerning you!

See you soon.

Love and Hugs, Mom

While his year proved to be challenging, our son rose to the challenge and persevered. As time progressed, he learned to be thankful for the opportunities before him and to trust God to help him overcome the difficulties. He grew to love the university, and his faith in God increased. God uses everything in our lives to draw us closer to Him. His greatest desire is for us to have unbroken fellowship and oneness with Him; it is why He created us.

As I look back over the years of my marriage and the raising of my children, it has become ever more apparent to me that all of my life is to be an analogy of my relationship with God through Christ. Our marriages are to be an example of Christ and the church. The way we love our children so unconditionally and would do anything for them, is just a small example of how much Christ loves us!

At this current stage in my life, I am on the horizon of an empty nest. Although all three of my children are still home, they are on the brink of leaving. They are more and more independent, less and less dependent upon us as parents. For a while, I struggled with feelings of sadness and wanting to turn back the clock. I let myself wallow in self-pity often enough; I also coveted the lives of younger moms just starting out or with small children at home. Self-pity is not God's will for anyone. God showed me this is sin. He showed me that the enemy wanted to keep me feeling sad and sorrowful about my life. If I remained in this state, I would be missing out on all of God's best for me right now in the present and in the future.

Instead, God helped me to see the blessings of this new and exciting season, one where my husband and I have more time to enjoy each other and to minister outside of our family circle. We always love spending time with our children. Our time together is still so much fun, but without the work and responsibility which were required when they were little. So, I am embracing this new season, full of possibilities and adventure.

My change of thinking was a process, and I am still growing in this area. Many days when I am in the house doing chores or in the car running errands, I listen to the Bible on my cell phone. I have also grown tremendously by reading Joyce Meyer's *Battlefield of the Mind* and by listening to her podcasts. Through the Word and through Joyce's teachings on the Word, I have been learning to take my thoughts captive.

One morning, my son and I had a disagreement, and for a little while the fellowship between us was broken. After prayer and both of us apologizing, our relationship was restored. However, as I was reflecting back upon the short time we were out of fellowship, I recalled the feelings of sadness and the longing to be restored. Isn't that how Christ views us? More than anything, He wants our fellowship and our love. He wants us to live every part of our life with Him, in the closest of friendships. As I think of my own kids leaving home, what saddens me most is the loss of the close daily fellowship we now enjoy. Now, don't get me wrong, I hope and pray that my children and I are always close in heart; however, having passed through the same stages they will be entering, I am also realistic. A new spouse followed by little children will be great blessings to them, and an answer to our lifelong prayers for our children. With those changes will also come the shifting of priorities, so they may focus on a new nuclear family. My husband and I will be left, just the two of us, to complete our life's journey together.

As we ponder this, we can feel sad at what has passed and will never be again, or we can be hopeful and joyful as we anticipate the new blessings that will come with in-laws and grandchildren. I have realized all of these stages of life, with their accompanying feelings, can give me a life picture of how God sees us. And isn't that truly the whole point of our lives? To love God and to glorify Him forever?

While I long for fellowship and conversation and time with my kids, God longs for the same with me. I am His kid, one of His favorites! He wants me to come to Him with my secret joys and deepest hurts, my hopes and my sorrows, my darkest fears, my longings and my dreams. He desires for me to have deeper and closer fellowship with Him. Prayer without ceasing. He longs for me to walk in constant conversation with Him, hearing His voice, doing the good works He reveals to me step-by-step. This kind of intimacy, even greater than that in a marriage, is His desire for us. We are His bride and He is the perfect bridegroom. He is the perfect father; we are His children and the blessed recipients of His unconditional love and favor.

As we lovingly remember past days with our younger children, these feelings can be turned back to God. We can realize that this is a small dose of His thoughts and feelings for us, and we can run to the always-ready arms of deep and satisfying fellowship with Him. I think that each and every stage of our lives gives us a life example, an analogy or allegory, of God's perfect plan for us. Instead of wallowing in sadness,

I am choosing to thank God for the wonderful memories and to thank Him for what I have learned from the difficult moments. As the Bible says, **"I press on toward the goal for the prize of the upward call of God in Christ Jesus" (Philippians 3:14).**

Our children need to see that we are seeking God and allowing Him to teach us, change us, and grow us. We are their real life in-the-flesh example, and we must model an active and vibrant faith for our children. Our kids need to see that we read the Bible regularly and apply it to our lives. God's Word is powerful and life-changing. If we model a love of the Bible for our children and spend time alone and with them in the Word, they will grow to love and depend upon it too.

In addition to reading God's Word, we need to spend time in prayer. Cultivating an ongoing discussion with the Lord is something I continue to work on. Prayer can simply be talking to God and listening expectantly for Him to speak to us through His Word, our thoughts, the words or actions of others, and examples in nature. For me, journaling has been a very helpful tool. I have also benefited greatly from Virkler's *Dialogue with God.*

Speaking the Word out loud is a powerful weapon against the enemy. When Jesus was tempted by the devil in the wilderness, He quoted scriptures aloud to come against him. We can read the Bible, pray, and quote scripture out loud. I am just beginning to see the great power and effect this can have on my own life and on the lives of my family members. God's Word has the power to change us!

We need to keep asking God for wisdom and to be continually filled with the Holy Spirit. If we ask, He promises to give us both of these things. The Bible says, **"But if any of you lacks wisdom, let him ask of God, who gives to all generously and without reproach, and it will be given to him" (James 1:5).** It also states, **"If you then, being evil, know how to give good gifts to your children, how much more will your heavenly Father give the Holy Spirit to those who ask Him?" (Luke 11:13).** I am trying to do this on a daily basis and am excited to see the amazing things God will do in my life and in the lives of my husband, my children, and others.

As we seek to love God above all and spend time with Him, we will be changed. Instead of striving or trying to change by our own will power, we can spend time abiding in God's presence and asking Him to do the work in us. He will change us little by little and will equip us to meet the challenges of each new day. As we meditate on His Word and focus our thoughts on Him, our minds will be transformed and we will become more like our wonderful heavenly Father.

His Help Meet

When my children entered their teen years and I entered my 40's, I began to realize that my time as a homeschooling mom was rapidly coming to an end. As I prayed and reflected on this for a season, the Lord reminded me that my primary role was always and would continue to be that of help meet to my husband; not that of mother, teacher, housekeeper, or cook.

Since the beginning of creation, God has had a unique plan for both men and women. God assigned Adam his work in the garden *before* He created Eve. The Bible says, **"Then the Lord God took the man and put him into the garden of Eden to cultivate it and keep it" (Genesis 2:15).** After God created Adam and appointed him as caretaker of His creation, God declared that He would make a helper for him. The Bible says, **"Then the Lord God said, 'It is not good for the man to be alone; I will make him a helper suitable for him'" (Genesis 2:18).** God created Eve to come alongside her man and help him in his work. As women, we will be most fulfilled when we joyfully embrace the role God intended for us. Serving as a helper to your husband does not imply that his life is more valuable or more important than yours. In no way does it mean that your hopes, dreams, and desires do not count. You are joint heirs in Christ! (see **Romans 8:17**). When we, as women, seek to serve and to help our husbands, we are acting in accordance with God's design.

Helping your husband will mean different things in every marriage. Each husband and each wife are unique individuals with their own talents, abilities, and preferences. **Ephesians 5:22** says, **"Wives, be**

subject to your own husbands, as to the Lord." Each wife is to submit to her *own* husband, not to the husband of her neighbor or best friend.

Our modern society has so warped and twisted God's original plan that men and women both are often confused as to their roles, and many are frustrated and unfulfilled as a result. If we follow God's design, presented to us in the Bible, our lives will take on the meaning and purpose He desires us to have.

On one of our overseas adventures, a faithful Christian woman gave me the book *Created to Be His Help Meet* by Debi Pearl. At the time, the book could only be ordered from their website (now it is widely available). As I poured over it night after night I felt a resounding, "Yes!" in my soul. Many of the principles she presented in her book were insights from the Bible that I had known deep inside but somehow could not organize into meaningful thoughts or actions. I rejoiced in ways I felt affirmed. I was convicted by ways I had failed. Amazed that God had flown me all the way to Europe to receive a book written in Tennessee, I thanked God for the tool He had given me.

When we arrived home from our travels, I immediately ordered a case of the books and gave them to other women as the Lord placed them on my heart. Sometimes they were joyfully received, other times they were rejected. I decided that I would just be obedient and leave the results up to God. With the Bible as my main guide, and the book as a secondary tool, I was better equipped to press on to become what God was calling me to be.

My first job is to seek to bless and to please my husband. He is the head of our home and as such, the weight of the responsibility falls on his shoulders. I am so thankful that I do not have to carry that load! But, as his helper I seek to find ways to encourage him and help him be all God created him to be. As the Bible says, **"…so that they may encourage the young women to love their husbands, to love their children, to be sensible, pure, workers at home, kind, being subject to their own husbands, so that the word of God will not be dishonored"** **(Titus 2:4,5).**

I clearly remember one particular year where I was put to the test. We had lost our main retail worker of 14 years and were having trouble replacing her. I was called upon to work in our store each Thursday, Friday, and Saturday. That year, our youngest was six years old, a little first grader. I felt so guilty since I could only help my children with school Monday through Wednesday. The other two days, they had to be self-motivated and work from their planners with little help from Mom. Fortunately, our store is right on our farm, so they could still find me if needed. But, the guilt persisted.

The summer prior to that year, my husband and I had listened to a series of homeschool teaching tapes recorded by a Christian homeschool father, Chris Davis. They challenged us to see each child as an individual that God had created with unique talents, gifts, and struggles. Our job was to help our children see the "way they were created to go," and to structure our home accordingly. We were convinced that our school needed to be different. We prayed that God would make it different. Little did we know He would answer so quickly and in the way He did.

After struggling with resentment and guilt, I was reminded that God was still in control. My husband wanted me to help him with the store. I knew I was doing the right thing and could rest in the fact that God had placed my husband in authority over our family. So, I continued to pray for my husband to have wisdom and discernment, for my kids to be okay, and for new help in the store. The following verses served as encouragement to me: **"Consider it all joy, my brethren, when you encounter various trials, knowing that the testing of your faith produces endurance. And let endurance have its perfect result, so that you may be perfect and complete, lacking in nothing"** (James 1:2-4). Despite the difficult circumstances, I trusted in God's faithfulness to His Word.

As it turned out, that year was a difficult one, but one that produced great fruit in our family. All of our children had to help in new ways, from answering phone calls and working in the store to taking on responsibility and care of the animals and of our home. They developed new skills and the confidence which accompanies the knowledge that they were really contributing to the family in tangible ways. Our youngest had not been quite ready to learn to read. The next year, when we had more help and I had more time, I worked with him on phonics and he picked it right up.

The new level of help the children were providing continued, and still continues to this day. They have learned to manage inventory, speak to customers, work a cash register and credit card machine, take phone orders, budget their time, and a host of other practical life skills, which will serve them well in their future. In addition to these general skill sets, they have also mastered some unique ones which provide them with a sense of accomplishment and some interesting things to converse with others about such as: caring for pigs, chickens, and cows; castrating steer; making ham, bacon, sausages, jerky, and meat products; making and aging cheeses; operating skid steers, tractors, mowers, and all sorts of farm equipment; welding, building, and fabricating; and the list goes on.

Although we all worked hard that year, we did it together and it helped create stronger family bonds. We needed each other. God, in His sovereignty, used the circumstances to produce lasting fruit. Would we have chosen the trials? No, but is it ever easy to willingly choose a more difficult path?

My mother's heart struggled that year, but I submitted to my husband as the final authority. I can now joyfully say that God did use it all for good. I am thankful He carried us through and gave us all we needed. God is so faithful and so good. He always takes care of His children!

In Debi Pearl's book *Created to Be His Help Meet*, she outlines three main types of men as compared to the Trinity: God the Father, God the Son, and God the Holy Spirit. Pearl maintains that men are created in the image of God which means they all carry aspects of His personality. She names the three types of men as Command (Father), Visionary (Holy Spirit), and Steady (Son), and claims that most men have one dominant characteristic while usually exhibiting some characteristics of all three. If you have a chance to read her book, I highly recommend it.

A brief and partial summary of her thoughts are as follows:

The Command Man is dominant, aggressive, somewhat bossy by nature, and likes to organize and delegate. He often "sees the bigger picture" or a more distant goal. A wife to this type of man can best help him by verbally expressing admiration and gratitude and by being ready to complete tasks he requests of her cheerfully and diligently. If not honored, obeyed, or reverenced, this type of man can feel disrespected and hurt.

The Visionary Man loves new ideas and confrontation. He feels the "need to communicate" his thoughts, feelings, and ideas. He tends to become extremely focused on his latest project or idea, and he wants his wife and children to work alongside of him and share his visions. A wife to this type of husband can best help him by being willing to follow his leading, by joyfully participating in his adventures, and by being prudent, flexible, objective and supportive. If his wife does not follow him, believe in him, or enthusiastically participate in his dreams with him, a Visionary can feel abandoned or hurt.

The third type, or Steady Man, is probably the most common. He is "not given to extremes," avoids controversy, "quietly ignores hypocrisy in others," and is "balanced and stable." To best help a Steady husband, his wife can practice thankfulness and gratitude, "not trying to change him" or to push him. She can fill her time with productive pursuits. The Steady Man is most hurt by a lack of thanksgiving or appreciation from his wife.

God created all men to lead. Respect his position before God, pray for him, and encourage him, but be careful not to take the reins. This is especially tempting for wives of a Steady Man (75-94).

This is by no means a complete summary of Debi Pearl's writing on this topic; however, it is a very helpful snapshot that can give us ideas as to how to best help our own husbands.

My husband is a very strong visionary type. The children and I have always been "on-call" to assist him with his newest project or business idea. When he prayerfully decided God called him to learn to make cheese in addition to all of the meat products he already made for our store, my husband needed our help with obtaining licenses, making cheese cloths out of muslin, running for needed supplies, etc.

I have generally avoided committing to too many outside activities because I never know when I might need to drop everything and run an errand or assist him in some way. Sometimes I may need to pick up supplies, bring flat tires to the station for repair, send an email, or make a delivery.

All that said, my husband is very supportive of any interests and activities of mine. If I make plans to do something, he is very encouraging and helpful. When I planned field trips with other homeschool moms, he would not ask me to do any errands that would interfere with our plans. If I wanted to take a long run to get some needed exercise and time alone, he would watch the children so that I could go. I don't want to imply that I do not have freedom to pursue activities or ministries the Lord leads me to pursue. I endeavor to be a good helper to my husband. He counts on me, confides in me, trusts me, cherishes me, and calls me "his beautiful bride." He seeks to love me as Christ calls him to. Adapting my schedule to his is something I do to honor him and to show him that I am willing to follow his lead. In turn, God has blessed us with a very happy and fulfilling marriage.

Study your husband. Ask God to show you ways to bless and encourage him. You may not need to be actively involved in his work in any way; however, you can listen to him talk about his day, pray for him, and express thankfulness for his hard work. Study the Bible (**Titus 2** is a great chapter for wives). The way you help your husband will not look the same for you as it does for anyone else. Be the best wife and friend to him you can be and trust God to show you the way.

In respecting your husband, you are obeying God's Word: **"Nevertheless, each individual among you also is to love his own wife even as himself, and the wife must see to it that she respects her husband" (Ephesians 5:33).** God clearly states that a wife is to respect her husband. If God commands it, He expects us to do it and He will give us the ability to do what He asks. Respect is a choice. Your husband does not need to deserve your respect in order for you to give respect to him. Regardless of your past, you can choose to respect your husband in thought, word, and deed, beginning today.

As you model respect for your husband before your children, they will learn to respect him as well. In doing so, they will be following God's command in the Bible which says, **"Honor your father and mother (which is the first commandment with a promise), so that it may be well with you, and that you may live long on the earth"** (Ephesians **6:2,3).** By honoring and respecting your husband, and by teaching your children to do the same, your family and your homeschooling will be blessed.

Allow Your Husband to Lead as God Directs

Many wives seem to have certain expectations as to how their husbands should be leading the family, spiritually, emotionally, and practically speaking. Desiring to have a Christ honoring home, a happy marriage, and joyful children are wonderful and biblical goals. Placing unrealistic demands or expectations on our husbands to single-handedly provide everything we wish for is unrealistic and possibly detrimental. Your husband's leadership may look different than you expect it to, and that is okay. Pray for him, and ask God to give him wisdom. Respect and honor him in thought, word, and deed, and think positively. Then, trust God to hear and answer your prayers.

When our children were little and we had just started our homeschool journey, I remember thinking that my husband should be leading our children in Bible reading and some type of formal devotions. I suppose this idea came from reading homeschool books or articles about other families and perhaps comparing our family to those about whom I was reading. Oh, the dangers of comparing and of discontented thinking!

Thankfully, God showed me that the way my husband was leading us did not look exactly like I thought it would look, but that it was good. I needed to adjust my expectations, choosing to see the good things and be thankful for them, rather than seeing what I perceived to be lacking.

My husband has never particularly enjoyed reading, and he especially dislikes reading aloud. He is exceptionally talented in so many areas, but this area is not his specific strength. I, on the other hand, have always loved to read aloud and find it easy and enjoyable. When I was only about eight years old, I was asked to read some scriptures in a chapel service at the prep school where my father was a science teacher. I remember loving it, and I wasn't the least bit nervous. I read aloud to my fourth-grade students when I was a public school teacher; I read books aloud to my husband as we traveled in the car; and I read to my own children throughout the day and before bedtime. Clearly, it would make sense that I should be the one to read the Bible out loud to our children. My husband was not relinquishing his role as spiritual leader of our home simply because he was not the one doing the reading.

As I prayed about how to train our children in the Bible, it was clear to me that I should make sure that reading the Bible was the priority of our homeschool day. Before starting any other homeschool subjects, I read the Bible out loud and prayed with our children. Often we recited verses out loud that we had decided to memorize. I felt good knowing that God had the top spot of our homeschool days. I also took comfort in knowing that I was honoring my husband by taking the time to read the Bible with our children. Although I was the one reading the Bible and instructing our children in a somewhat formal manner, my husband was still our spiritual leader and was excellent in weaving God into every part of our lives.

For example, one day as he sat outside with our children, my husband pointed out a Mulberry tree. A few months earlier he had mentioned a desire to remove the sapling of a tree, but life had been busy and the tree remained. Now, the Mulberry sapling had become a substantial tree, requiring much more effort and possibly a tractor for its removal. He went on to share with the children that sin in our lives was much the same as that tree. If we allowed God to remove the sin in our lives when He first revealed it to us, it would be much easier than if we allowed it to grow and to take root.

Often, real life examples like this one would come up in life on the farm, and my husband would weave them naturally into the conversation. Thankfully, I realized that this was his way of leading us spiritually. It was so much better for us because my husband was operating in his gifts rather than through some preset formula. Each husband and father is equipped with different gifts and personality styles. Our job is to look for the best in him and encourage him to lead our families as God directs him to.

In addition to yielding to our husband's spiritual leadership, we need to learn to yield to his leadership in practical areas as well. Let me use vacation planning as an example. I am more cautious, and more of a planner than my husband. If it had been up to me, we probably would have decided on a potential vacation spot, planned for the trip, saved the necessary funds, and then we would have gone. One year, my husband, who spends a lot of time each day listening quietly to the Lord for direction, discerned that we should go to France for our month-long vacation. A friend had offered us the use of his house and after my husband had prayed about it, he believed we were supposed to go.

I immediately felt anxious. *A month in France! How much would it cost? What would we do there? Would our kids like it? Would we be safe?* We had never taken all of our children overseas and this would be a very big trip. Although my initial reaction was one of fear and trepidation more than excitement, I have learned to work through these feelings. I pray and tell God that I trust Him to lead my husband, then I hold on for the ride and enjoy the adventure.

When my husband discerned we should go to New Zealand one year, and another year to Nicaragua, I went through a similar process to prepare myself and the kids to go and to embrace the journey. Now some of you may be thinking I am crazy. Perhaps you would absolutely LOVE for your husband to come home and announce that you would be taking a month-long trip to a faraway place, any place. I get it. I feel incredibly blessed; however, for me these trips have often stretched me way beyond my comfort zone. No one usually thrills at first to the thought of discomfort, and I am no exception. Each of us is wired differently. One person's dream can be another person's nightmare and vice versa.

Looking back, I can see how correct my husband's discernment was. Our kids were the perfect ages to travel when we took those trips. They loved being together as a family and embraced the adventure. We have wonderful memories and have learned a great deal about the world. Now that our kids are older and have busy lives of their own, it is difficult to find time to all get away together. We truly went on those trips at the perfect time, in God's time, and I am so grateful.

Now that we have been married over 30 years, I have seen God lead my husband over and over again. I am thankful for how he listens to the Lord, and I have come to trust his discernment and follow his lead. I have even improved in my initial reaction when he tells me of our next adventure! Although I still have many areas in which I seek to grow, I am thankful that I have made progress!

Following my husband's lead in financial matters has probably been the most difficult area for me. I grew up with wonderful Christian parents who provided me with love and encouragement, and I am so very thankful for them. Both my mother and my father were the first in their respective families to become Christians. They did not have the example of Christian parents to follow, but I think they did a wonderful job in raising their children. All three of us have followed Christ from a young age and have married God-loving Christian spouses. I want to be sure that I always honor my parents as God commands. Like any parents, they were not perfect. My father usually expressed concern and uncertainty over our finances. Because he was my provider, I picked up on that anxiety and have had to work with the Lord to overcome it little by little.

My husband never frets over finances. He is by nature a visionary and a risk-taker. Thankfully, he is a smart businessman and more importantly, an obedient disciple of God. When we were first married, he declared that we were purchasing a smokehouse for our butcher shop. I remember thinking it cost as much as a Mercedes! Of course, it was the right decision and the smokehouse allowed us to make delicious ham, bacon, kielbasa, and other smoked products, which helped grow our business. Over the years there have been many business investments: tractors, meat grinders, vacuum seal machines, building additions, and a cheese plant.

Did you hear that, a cheese plant?! That month-long trip to France became the impetus for our cheese business. Apparently, my husband dreamed of making cheese for *a while*. This was unknown to me. After returning from our trip to France and Switzerland, where we had observed and toured several cheese operations, he had been praying about making cheese. Of course, he had not let me in on his ponderings until he became sure God was leading him. To me it seemed shocking. *Make cheese?! What?* But he had prayed about it and felt sure God wanted him to make cheese.

So, we met with a cheese consultant, ordered equipment, decided on types of cheeses to make, built a cheese making room and a cheese aging room, and we made cheese, all within three months of returning home from our trip! Once again, when the dust settled, I could see God's hand in my husband's leadership. The cheese was delicious; our customers loved it; and six years after making our initial batch, our cheese placed second in the nation at the American Cheese Society competition!

One year we took the family to an international meat convention in Germany. Upon returning, my husband decided that THIS was the year to purchase a very expensive packaging machine. This time, he mentioned the machine previously, so I knew that SOMEDAY it would probably become a reality in our butcher shop. Apparently, the time was now. (Do you see how dangerous these vacation trips can be? I always joke about it, but vacations do provide my husband with ample thinking and prayer time, which usually lead to new adventures or acquisitions). True to form, this was the year.

In our butcher shop, we process deer for hunters. When they harvest a deer, we cut it up and make numerous delicious products from the venison. The year that we purchased our new packaging machine, we processed nearly 2600 deer during the hunting season, 700 more than the previous year! The new machine cut our packaging time by seventy-five percent. We ran the machine all day and could keep up with demand. Without it, we would have been up late at night or we would have been scrambling to hire more help. God is so good! I am pleased to say that I did not even lose a night of sleep being anxious about the purchase. As I keep seeking God, He is faithfully changing me.

I could give example after example of ways my husband has led, and I have followed (not always as cheerfully, or optimistically as I could have, but I am making great progress), and we have seen clear evidence that it was God leading us all along.

Now, I do not mean to imply that my husband's discernment is perfect or that I follow his lead perfectly. We are both human, and we are both imperfect and sinful. When I do feel I disagree with a decision, or feel as if I am discerning something differently than my husband is, I speak up and share that with him. We discuss it and pray about it. I continue to pray that God gives him wisdom, and he prays as well. Sometimes, my husband has decided to change course, but sometimes he has still felt he should go through with his initial decision. Either way, I have learned to trust God. I know that He will work all things out for our good, even though we will make mistakes along the way.

I have not yet arrived, but as Paul says, I keep pressing on (see **Philippians 3:13,14**). God continues to work in us and through us as we submit to Him. I am so thankful that He is such a patient teacher.

There are several special Christian homeschool moms in my life whom I feel privileged to call friends. They have been called to follow their husbands as well, and each of their circumstances is completely unique. One friend, the mother of eight precious children, is married to a steadier type of husband. Due to some financial hardships, they have lived in a tiny house with three bedrooms for many years. Instead of vacations, she has planned stay-cations with week-long lists of inexpensive memory-making family activities. She has made her small home as cozy and full of love and joy as possible. Would she have loved to trade places with me and travel to France? Perhaps. But, she has chosen to be content.

Her days consist of loving her husband and children, homeschooling, planning and preparing meals, overseeing household chores, and serving her family and others. I am fairly certain she has not had to lop legs off of deer carcasses, assist in cheese making, or drop everything to chase cows that have escaped from the pasture. Would I have loved to trade places with her at times? Perhaps. But, I am choosing contentment as well. To me, this beautiful lady embodies **Philippians 4:11**, which reads: **"Not that I speak from want, for I have learned to be content in whatever circumstances I am."** She chooses joy. Her face is radiant. She is a loving and patient mother. Her children have followed her lead and are some of the kindest and most joyful children I know. She is one of my heroes!

Another beautiful mother of four is married to a naval officer. They have moved every three years for their entire married life. She has parented alone for months at a time while he has bravely served tours in Afghanistan and Iraq. While her husband was away, she and the children would Skype with him and keep their family connected in heart. Her husband has trusted her to care for the children and home and make daily decisions in his absence. When her husband returned home, she has learned to turn the reins back over to him. She has prayed for him as they have made decisions regarding where to live and whether to send their kids to school or keep them home. God continues to bless their family as they seek Him.

A third dear Christian sister is the mother of five young men. For a period of about four years, she cared for her husband's ill mother in their home. For those years, my usually social and outgoing friend was often confined to her home and her mother-in-law's care schedule. In following her husband's lead, she honored his mother as she sacrificially cared for her. Her children witnessed this wonderful example of serving and they, too, had numerous opportunities to learn to serve alongside their parents. This season has passed for her, but the rewards of her faithfulness will surely continue.

For each wife, following her husband's lead will look different. As I share these stories, don't compare them to yours; instead, ask God to reveal His heart to you and allow Him to lead you as you follow your husband. Keep your marriage as your top priority after your relationship with the Lord. Then, when your children are grown, you will find yourself with a rich heritage, wonderful memories, and precious family relationships that you share with your very best friend. One of the best gifts you can give to your children is a loving and stable marriage.

Remember:
- Seek God first.
- Make your husband your next priority.
- Respect him.

- Pray for your husband to have wisdom in all of his decisions.
- Pray for yourself to have wisdom.
- Communicate.
- Choose thankfulness.
- Trust God.

Train up a Child

Behold, children are a gift of the Lord, the fruit of the womb is a reward.

Psalms 127:3

Parenting is a great adventure! Just as marriage is a living example of how we are the bride of Christ, becoming a parent makes us realize how much our Heavenly Father loves us, cares for us, and seeks to teach us and give us what is for our ultimate good. The love you have for your children will continue to grow as you train them up in the Lord. The thought of God giving up His Only Son for us becomes an even more incredible revelation!

Training children is a full-time job, and it is vital to remember the child's heart, not just his external behavior, is the focus. For this incredibly important task, we need to ask God for His wisdom. As the Bible says, **"But if any of you lacks wisdom, let him ask of God, who gives to all generously and without reproach, and it will be given to him" (James 1:5).**

As we seek God, He will guide us in training up our children: **"Trust in the Lord with all your heart and do not lean on your own understanding. In all your ways acknowledge Him, and He will make your paths straight" (Proverbs 3:5, 6).**

God has created each one of us, and each one of our children, to walk our own unique path. We have different gifts, varied talents and abilities, and particular callings. It is important to seek the Lord as we direct our children, and it is essential to train them to hear God's voice for themselves as they grow. We cannot worry about what others think; we must follow His leading. Each child is a unique individual who will need different training. The Bible says, **"Train up a child in the way he should go, even when he is old he will not depart from it" (Proverbs 22:6).** This verse teaches us that there is a specific way each child should go. As our children grow and we begin to see their particular gifts and talents, we can guide them to help them discover God's plan for their lives. If we help our children learn to operate in their gifts, they will find fulfillment and joy.

When our oldest was four years old, a dear family friend made the comment, "Remember, college isn't for everyone. For some people, that is their moral downfall." Now, college seemed forever away for our little boy, and I cannot even recall the context of that comment, but for some reason, it stuck with me. I believe it was part of the beginning of the journey the Lord was preparing us for. A year and a half later, when we officially began our homeschooling, our oldest made it clear that he did not enjoy academics in their own right; for him, learning needed to be hands-on and practical, for a purpose.

We tried to make our school as real and active for him as possible. We used a felt board for Bible stories, chanted our memory verses together, and sometimes acted out Bible scenes. For math, we used plenty of manipulatives, memorized math facts while bouncing on Hoppity-hops, wrote checks to pay household bills, and completed special grocery shopping math lessons. In addition to this, there was still the much dreaded math page which was necessary to incrementally develop needed skills. History was read aloud together and often followed by a discussion, a coloring page, a composition, or an activity. Some favorite activities were making a castle and our own coat-of-arms shields, constructing the Nile River and model pyramids, and writing in hieroglyphics. We usually tried to tie our writing and literature into whatever we were studying in history and science. Science was an easy subject to make hands-on. We took nature walks and painted watercolor scenes of what we observed. We dissected owl pellets, worked with gears and electric circuit kits, flew paper airplanes and small hot air balloons, visited science museums, harvested our own honey, made our own cheese, and worked with farm animals.

We completed Bible study, science, art, music, and history together. Each child completed his own reading and writing assignments independently. As I look back, I especially treasured our times of reading aloud and discussing our reading together. By weaving our history and science into our reading and our writing, the learning seemed more relevant to our children. Although I thought we tried to make learning as fun and relevant as possible, our oldest still always claimed to greatly dislike school. Ah, so humbling!

Plenty of time was also spent on chores. After schoolwork was completed, each child had a list of chores on the refrigerator, which was to be completed before having free time. On a farm, there are lots of chores! We had household chores like vacuuming, making beds, taking out the trash, and emptying the dishwasher. Then, there were outside chores of checking the animal water, feeding the pigs and chickens, gathering eggs, driving tractors, and putting away hay. Lastly, we had work to do in our shop, where the kids learned to package items, take phone orders, and wait on customers.

As our children grew, we tried to encourage their strengths and work on their weaknesses, praying that God would reveal their own paths to them. Around age thirteen, our oldest asked me if we were doing "enough" to prepare him for college. This sentence came from the same child who always wanted to finish schoolwork as soon as possible! He claimed he might like to go to college in Texas or go to Penn State when the time came. By about the age of fifteen, he had changed his mind and declared that he did not want to go to college after all, but wanted to continue in the family business.

Now, some of you may think, "What does a fifteen-year-old know? How could he possibly know what he wants to do at this point in life?" I can understand your thinking, but we knew our son. He had always been very focused and determined when he set his mind on something. Once, when he was around five, he spent over two hours chasing a butterfly. He passed on lunch and continued hunting down that butterfly until he finally caught it.

Because we now knew what was in his heart to do, we could plan his high school years accordingly. Instead of calculus, he studied accounting.

In place of chemistry, he learned meat science. We worked out his schedule so he could complete his schoolwork in four days, leaving two days to work in our shop and learn by apprenticeship. After high school graduation, he began working full-time and taking classes part-time at the community college. To us, this seemed like the perfect road for him: lots of hands-on work and a minimal amount of schoolwork, which was just enough to supplement him with some needed business skills for the future.

Our daughter decided she would like to finish school early. She desired, most of all, to someday become a wife and mother. Her high school studies included home economics, sewing, and reading books about God's role for women as wives and mothers. In addition, she completed the necessary academics that would prepare her for college if that was where she was led. As we all prayed about her future plans, she became interested in the nursing field. She loved the elderly and decided she would enjoy learning to care for their needs. After researching a bit, our daughter decided she would find what she needed in a one-year practical nursing program at our community college, where she could earn her LPN in just twelve months, debt-free. Fueled with a new plan, she completed two high school years in one and graduated a year early. At age seventeen she was accepted into the nursing program.

Nearly everyone we talked to advised our daughter that she should, in fact, enroll in a four-year college and earn her bachelor's degree in nursing. Everywhere we turned, we received the same friendly advice. Our daughter began to grow distressed. She wavered in her decision and came to us for frequent discussions. Finally, one day my husband told her, "Honey, if God is telling you to do this LPN program and you have a peace about it, then that is what you should do. It doesn't matter if the whole world is telling you something different. You do what is in your heart to do, and Mom and I will support you." With that, it was as if someone lifted a giant boulder off her shoulders. She excitedly enrolled in the one-year program.

Her year proved to be very challenging and intense, but our daughter rose to the challenge, making top marks in every class. She enjoyed her classmates, who ranged in age from twenty-three to forty-eight.

At the end of the year, she was asked by her classmates to give the commencement address, which she did. The entire year was a wonderful and positive growing experience.

Following graduation, our daughter immediately passed her boards and was hired for a full-time position at a local nursing home. After several months, she decided she missed working in our shop and asked if she could come back part-time and work as a substitute at a different nursing facility. We were thrilled! She joyfully embraced her two part-time jobs, which also allowed her to have more time to help out at home and on the farm. Her flexible schedule allowed her to travel to Kenya for a mission trip and attend church retreats and other functions that came up.

Several years later, our daughter decided she did not love being a nurse, but really loved working in our business. She came back to work full-time for us and became our retail manager, taking on many of my responsibilities. As I write this I am so thankful for all of the time we have had together. She and I do the grocery shopping and household chores together. One day she will get married and move away, but for now, I am treasuring our time.

Our youngest, during his senior of high school, was still unsure of exactly how God was leading him. He considered coming into the business but thought he might want to do something else. He felt the pull to possibly attend a four-year college, perhaps to study business, then come back with a new energy and perspective to run the business with his brother. He was restless and feeling the need to be away. During his junior and senior years, he took several basic classes at our local community college. If God did call him to go away to a four-year college, he would have some experience juggling college courses and would have some credits to start out. Through an interesting series of events, we all discerned that he was to attend a Christian college and study business. The following fall, he was the first to leave home for school.

We are confident that God will show him, in perfect time, exactly where he needs to be and when. The beauty of homeschooling is that we have the freedom to allow each of our children to follow their own path.

We can assist them, guide them, and provide them with opportunities for life experiences so that they can discern "the way in which they should go."

In their book, *I Saw the Angel in the Marble*, Chris and Ellyn Davis say:

> I believe that when God gives a child to parents, that child comes prepackaged with a set of giftings and callings uniquely his or her own. Inside that child is a seed, which if properly nourished, will grow up into the mature expression of what is within that seed. Just as simply as an acorn (which looks nothing like an oak tree) becomes an oak tree under the right conditions, so a child will (under the right conditions) grow up to become exactly the person his Father created him to be. (105)

As I was reading **Luke 8:22-26** (the passage where Jesus and his disciples are in the boat and Jesus falls asleep in the midst of a storm), the Lord gave me a different insight to this passage than I had seen ever before. Jesus said to his disciples, **"Let us go over to the other side of the lake."** His instructions were clear, the destination evident. The disciples understood the mission and launched out in faithful obedience. Jesus fell asleep, the wind and rain came, and the disciples became afraid. I am sure they felt alone, that Jesus was not there for them. But, all the time, He was there peacefully sleeping in the boat. They could not hear his voice, for it was silent. They felt they must "wake Jesus up" so He might help them. When they did, He rebuked them for their lack of faith.

While I pondered this passage, I prayed, "Lord, how many times have You set my course, and I have turned back or been fearful when I could no longer feel Your presence or hear Your voice? You were still in the boat with the disciples, but they did not trust You to protect them and bring them safely to their destination."

I believe that if we ask God to show us the destination, what we are aiming for in the lives of each of our children, He will tell us and point the way. He will guide us and walk with us, regardless of whether we "feel" Him or not. Our job is to listen, launch out in obedience, and trust Him to take us to our destination. God will be glorified in every step of the journey.

As my kids were growing up and I became distressed over what math curriculum we were using, or whether or not our kids were "behind" where they should be, I would try to step back and think of the big picture. When my kids left home, what qualities and skills did I want them to possess? First, I wanted them to be fully devoted disciples of Christ, who realized their salvation in Him and who loved Him above all as they sought to follow Him each day. Secondly, I wanted them to have the ability to make their way in this world when they were on their own.

This big picture thinking helped me remain focused on the ultimate destination and all of the smaller stepping stones along the way. Hardships will come. The enemy will try to discourage. If we keep seeking God, He will point us in the right direction and remain with us until we reach the other side of the lake.

CHAPTER 3

Life's Lessons Learned along the Way

Don't Compare!

I RECALL ONE OF the first few years of homeschool evaluations, which are required in the state of Pennsylvania for all homeschooled children ages eight through sixteen. An evaluation consists of a certified teacher interviewing the homeschooled child, checking their daily log (where academic days and activities are recorded), and looking through their portfolio (a collection of samples of their work in each academic area). After interviewing the child, the evaluator writes a letter to the school district certifying that the child is making progress and is receiving an appropriate education. My evaluator is a dear college friend. She and I, both certified teachers, had decided that each year we would "trade" and evaluate each other's children.

I remember evaluating her oldest son one year in particular. I looked through his portfolio stuffed to the brim with excellent compositions, stellar vocabulary and spelling, advanced math and science papers, and more than two hundred books on his independent reading list! I could feel my pulse quicken as fear gripped my heart. *Wow! Was I adequate for this job? Was I failing my own children? What was I thinking believing I was somehow qualified for this task?* I tried to focus on the child and portfolio before me as we chatted, and I took careful notes so that later I could type up an accurate evaluation.

As I wrote my notes, I fought off thoughts of my own inadequacies that continued to swirl around in my mind. *My son only read around fifteen books; we typed the list in a larger font so that it would fill the page. His writing seemed elementary compared to this scholar's compositions before me. His spelling was still a work in progress. Did I push him hard enough? Maybe I didn't give him enough encouragement.*

After my friend and I finished our interviews, we met at the kitchen table to rehash our year. We talked about our families, our lives, our homeschooling. What amazed me was that she did not criticize or point her finger at me, scolding me for knowing better and not doing a good enough job. Instead, she praised me. She found it amazing that my young son could remove an engine from a trash-picked mini bike and mount it on a go-cart all by himself. He could change the oil in the lawnmower, use power tools, wait on customers in our store, raise bees and harvest honey, drive tractors attached to hay wagons, and do a host of other practical and useful skills.

As I began to see him through her eyes, I realized that he really *had* learned a great deal. Maybe he did not read 200 books, but he could read well. Maybe he could not write like a high schooler, but he was still young and his writing showed progress. Maybe his spelling and handwriting needed improvement, but we were working on it. God showed me that day, and many days after, that each family was different and their schooling would look different, and it was okay. As a matter of fact, it was better than okay. It was wonderful! What freedom we have had in our homeschool experiences to teach our children as individuals and train them up "in the way they should go," in the way the Lord created them to be.

From that day forward, I chose to celebrate our differences and seek the Lord more for His plan for our children. My husband has wonderful discernment, and all along, he told me our kids were doing great, I was an awesome teacher and mom, and I should stop worrying. His constant encouragement and confidence in what we were doing gave me courage to press on in our family's way of homeschooling.

I think one of the biggest temptations of homeschool moms, and perhaps one of the primary steps down the road of discouragement, is the tendency to compare ourselves with others. *Wow! They have twelve children, sew their own clothes, bake their own bread, have beautiful well-behaved children, play in their own orchestra, score top grades on standardized tests, write books. Such feats might make our family seem plain and ordinary. I can barely keep up with the laundry and get meals on the table, my kids whine or argue, sometimes I totally lose my temper, our test scores are marginal, I feel frazzled and disorganized. Surely, I am the worst homeschool parent ever! Maybe my kids would be better off with another teacher!*

These are all lies that the enemy uses to undermine our confidence and soften our resolve. When we hear about something great or unique that a particular homeschool family is doing, we file that in our mental notebook of "Things We Should Be Doing in our Family/Homeschool." Another family is brought to our attention for another wonderful trait. This, too, gets filed. Eventually we have this imagined list of a perfect homeschool family in which everyone excels in every arena. Clearly, this is not possible, and it simply leads to discouragement. Instead, we need to cultivate a thankful heart, expressing praise for our own unique family and seeking God to guide us in the special path He has for us.

Often people have watched our family from afar and expressed admiration for how we all work together on our farm and in our business. From the time our children were small, they have had to help with the chores on the farm and they have been required to help out in the butcher shop as needed, especially in November and December. I am thankful for all of the opportunities they have had to learn life skills. They have learned how to work hard, even when it is not always fun, and they have learned what it means to work together as a family.

In the winter, we close our business and take a four to five-week vacation. God has blessed us with many unique opportunities to travel, both here in our wonderful country and abroad. Much of our time is spent traveling in our RV, visiting friends, and experiencing new adventures. I am thankful for all of the time we have had to both work and play together.

Perhaps if you observed us over a period of time, you might be tempted to add a family business and farm to that perfect family notebook. Remember that every positive usually has a counterpart.

What people do not seem to realize is that it is *a lot* of work. The children and I have stood outside in cold weather snipping the legs off deer that hunters bring in for processing. We spend most of the time between Thanksgiving and Christmas working in the shop then heading to bed after a long hard day. No baking Christmas cookies, or spending leisurely days singing carols and wrapping presents. We are answering phones, taking orders, waiting on customers, and trying to squeeze in Christmas preparations for our celebration. I am not saying this to complain; I am truly thankful that the Lord continually provides all that our family needs and more. What I have learned from my own experience is that while the grass may appear greener somewhere else, I need to walk in the path the Lord has prepared for me. Have I always done this willingly and joyfully? Unfortunately, I have to confess that at times I have been grumpy about having to work so hard for a season or have given in to self-pity. I have been short with the children and short on sleep.

Sometimes I have looked at other families and wished that my husband had a more usual job, that I did not have to work in the business, that our schedule was more predictable, that I could leisurely bake those Christmas cookies. God knows what is best for each one of us. He pulls us out of our comfort zones and stretches us each in different ways. He is the potter and we are the clay; He knows exactly what He is shaping. Trust God. Be content where you are. He knows the big picture, and He can be trusted!

God is still working on me. I have had to learn to practice thankfulness, to take every thought captive. As it says in the Bible, **"We are destroying speculations and every lofty thing raised up against the knowledge of God, and we are taking every thought captive to the obedience of Christ" (2 Corinthians 10:5).** Whatever I choose to think on, to play repeatedly in my head, is what takes root in my heart. I desire to choose joy and thankfulness, not bitterness, resentment, or self-pity. It is a daily, moment-by-moment choice. And, when I truly sit back and look at my life, I am overwhelmed with thankfulness at the goodness and blessing of the Lord.

I love the verses in **Hebrews 12:1,2: "Therefore, since we have so great a cloud of witnesses surrounding us, let us also lay aside every encumbrance and the sin which so easily entangles us, and let us run with endurance the race that is set before us, fixing our eyes on Jesus, the author and perfecter of faith."**

As a former high school and college hurdler, these are verses I can truly picture. In the 400 meter hurdles, every runner is assigned an individual lane in which she is required to stay for the entire race. The inside lane is staggered behind the next one to the right and so on, leading outward to the outermost lane, where the runner is staggered ahead of all the rest. The hurdles are spaced evenly around the track so that each runner has the same distance between hurdles, and each runner runs an equal distance.

Whenever I was in an inside lane, I could look at the runners in the lanes in front of me and see when they jumped their hurdles. If they took off the ground before I did, they were ahead of me in the race; if I took off first, I was ahead. By the time we all reached the final stretch of track, the hurdles were side by side and it was the exciting finale of the race.

It was often tempting to keep looking over into the other lanes to measure how I was doing; however, I found that I could run much faster if I kept my eyes focused on my own lane and on my next hurdle. If I glanced over at another runner during the race, I took my eyes off of my own obstacles and ran the risk of hitting a hurdle, tripping, or being disqualified for veering out of my lane. If I ran with all my strength and stayed focused, I could run a better time and maybe even be the first to break the tape at the finish line.

I need to keep my eyes focused on Jesus and on my "race." My lane may look different from yours. It may appear that I am running behind, or not running as well as I could be. I may even trip and fall. But, if I keep pressing on towards the finish line, God will run beside me to help me and cheer me on. He gives me my lane assignment, and I need to be faithful to complete my race to the best of my ability, relying on Him for strength and wisdom.

While I sometimes still struggle with the temptation to compare, I have learned to quickly take any negative thoughts captive. The Bible teaches us: **"Whatever is true, whatever is honorable, whatever is right, whatever is pure, whatever is lovely, whatever is of good repute, if there is any excellence and if anything worthy of praise, dwell on these things" (Philippians 4:8).** Choosing to think on all things positive and good will help each of us to run our race well.

One area in which homeschool moms are tempted to compare is in the arena of co-ops. For those of you unfamiliar with the term, a cooperative, or co-op, is simply a group of homeschoolers who get together and divide the children up into groups so that one or more of the parents teach or supervise each group. Co-ops can be as simple as one or two moms getting together twice a month for social purposes to very complex co-ops offering numerous classes and subjects for grades K-12 each week.

Our family participated in co-ops to a small degree. When our kids were very young we participated in a co-op that included around 10 families. My youngest was in a preschool room where I assisted a teacher. Mostly, the kids played and we did a few crafts. My older two attended a class on the human body and a drama class, which culminated in a short play. I think the co-op lasted about 8 weeks or so. That was the only time we attended a larger cooperative.

At one point, one other mom and I traded off teaching every other week; she taught art while I planned science lessons. A few years later, two other moms and I had a bi-monthly co-op where we learned art, music, and physical education. These co-ops were informal and provided some fun social time for the kids, as well as for the moms. The content of the classes was supplemental to what we were teaching at home, but did not place any additional burdens on the kids for completing assignments or preparing ahead for future lessons.

My favorite co-op experiences spanned a period of about eight years. A dear friend and I sat down each summer and created a list of field trips for the school year. We planned one per month. The nice thing about working with just one other family is that we could adjust the dates as needed and the logistics were easier than with a larger group. Some of my children's fondest memories are of these trips with our close family friends. We even took some camping and overnight trips with the both of our families.

For us, this was the extent of our co-op experiences. Because our business is so busy in November and December and because we take a month-long vacation in the late winter, co-ops did not work for our family. Most co-ops run from September through May and we could never commit to such a long period of time.

My close college friend, our homeschool evaluator, lives in an area with an abundance of homeschoolers. She has participated in very large co-ops as well as private classes (which require a fee), and her children have taken classes in cooking, writing, British literature, chemistry, algebra, physical education, drama, and numerous other subjects. Her children have all excelled academically, and the co-ops and extra classes provided them with an excellent and challenging education.

Co-ops can be a great addition to a homeschool curriculum; however, participation in them can cause some problems if entered blindly. First, co-ops can defeat the whole purpose of *home*schooling. I have witnessed families running around from one activity to the next. The frenzied pace and the agenda of the co-op determine the family's curriculum and schedule. Family time is eroded. Stress is increased. The temptation to compare becomes stronger.

Homeschooling can at times feel like a lonely path. When homeschool mothers get together, they are often tempted to compare how their own children "measure up" to the rest in the group. A woman's self-worth can be closely tied to the job she is doing as homeschool mother and teacher. Because of this, there is the danger of co-ops becoming a competition, judging who has the most kids, the best behaved kids, the most advanced or talented kids, etc.

I am grateful we were only able to participate in the co-ops I described above. Although I was not subjected frequently to the temptation of comparisons within a co-op, I had enough struggles in my own mind and heart with comparing myself to other moms and comparing my children with other children.

Facebook and social media can also become a snare if we allow ourselves to compete and compare. We need to beware of becoming prideful about our own lives or critical of the lives of others. We don't need to judge other moms to make ourselves look or feel better. Our worth comes from Christ alone, as do our gifts and talents.

Comparing ourselves, our lives, our marriages, our children, or our lifestyles with others can easily lead into the sin of covetousness. It is one thing to look at a situation and evaluate it for the purposes of growing in the Lord. It is quite another to look and wish you had what someone else does. "Covet" means to wish, long, or crave for. One of God's ten commandments includes the directive, **"You shall not covet" (Exodus 20:17)**. I know that I need to remind myself that coveting is a sin, and I frequently need to reign in my thoughts and take them captive. When I am tempted to compare or to covet, I try to turn my heart to thanksgiving for all the Lord has given me. I need to run my own race and run it well.

God has been teaching me that I need to embrace *my* story. He has a special plan for each of us, a part in eternity He wants us to fulfill. God has given each of us and each of our children different talents and abilities, and it is up to us to choose to use them for His glory. God is the potter, and we are the clay. As the Bible says, **"On the contrary, who are you, O man, who answers back to God? The thing molded will not say to the molder, 'Why did you make me like this,' will it? Or does not the potter have a right over the clay, to make from the same lump one vessel for honorable use and another for common use?" (Romans 9: 20,21)**. We each need to learn to be content and flourish wherever God places us.

Our job is to use the talents we have been given to serve our God, to be a help meet to our husbands, and to train up our children in the way God has for them. He has given us our abilities, whether great or small. As it says in the Bible, **"For it is just like a man about to go on a journey, who called his own slaves and entrusted his possessions to them. To one he gave five talents, to another, two, and to another, one, each according to his own ability; and he went on his journey" (Matthew 25: 14,15)**. We honor God by giving Him our best, and we can trust Him with the results. It is tempting to look around and wish parts of our lives were different, tempting to covet, tempting to want to rewind and redo, but we must keep our eyes on Jesus so that we do not miss our own path. God forgives, redeems, restores, and weaves it all into *our* story. Embrace *your* story. Remember, only you can live your life. Live it well!

Remember:

Lesson: Don't Compare! Thank God for the unique family that you have.

Action: Take your thoughts captive. Meditate on God's Word and the "good" things in life. Practice thankfulness. Make a list of all the ways God has made your family special. Perhaps you are talented in music, athletics, or the arts. Maybe you have a special ministry to a needy family, or your house is where all the teenagers like to come and hang out. Embrace your part in God's story.

Don't Let Fear Steal your Joy!

We were sitting on our bed as a family, watching an interesting show on Animal Planet. My heart felt strange. It seemed to be fluttering, then flip-flopping around in my chest. *Surely it would stop in a minute; everyone has occasional beat irregularities.* After a couple minutes, I said something about it, and my oldest son put his ear to my chest. He proclaimed, "Mommy, that doesn't sound right!" My husband and children placed hands on me and prayed for me. We finished watching the program. Then I went to bed, trying to forget about it.

In the middle of the night, I woke up, heart racing, and out of breath. *Am I having a heart attack?* I awakened my husband, and we headed for the emergency room. And so began a new medical journey in our lives. I was diagnosed with atrial fibrillation; basically, the top portion of my heart was misfiring electrically and causing a totally irregular pulse. This condition itself is not life threatening, but the risk for stroke is present if the irregular beats continue. No underlying cause or problem was discovered. After three days in the hospital, I was sent home with a couple of medications. My heart beat was mostly regular on the medication, but it still often felt "funny," and it seemed as if I was aware of every beat.

Looking back, I truly believe that stress and fear contributed to my medical condition. Prior to the hospitalization, the following events occurred in the span of three months:

- A family trip to New Zealand-a month traveling in a rented RV (an incredible blessing, but a change and a stress).
- The passing of my mother-in-law-a truly wonderful woman, one I hope to be like.
- Easter-holidays are always busy and stressful. We sell meat, which is what almost everyone eats for a holiday.
- Family flu-one by one we all got it-high fevers and respiratory troubles.
- Lice-yuck! Need I say more?!
- Missed period for two weeks-could I be pregnant again at age forty?!

As I reflected on the idea that my condition was stress induced, it also occurred to me that it had a spiritual dimension. I am not implying that every physical condition is a result of something spiritual. However, in my case, I believed it was a spiritual attack fueled by fear. I would wake up in the night out of the blue with my heart racing and adrenaline pulsing through my body. Fear and heaviness were upon me. I would get up, read my Bible, then pray. Sometimes I would wake my husband to pray for me. Eventually, it would be as if everything lifted, and I could sleep again.

You may think I am crazy. I have to be honest; before this happened to me I used to be skeptical about people who claimed to have panic attacks. Boy did this teach me not to judge!

The more I reflected on the role of fear in my life, the more I realized it had plagued me from adolescence on. Fear, anxiety, worry, whatever you want to call it, was there robbing me of the joy of the present. I started to think back on my fears: bad grades, failing a test, not finding friends in college, college work load, finding a husband, teaching, having the principal observe my class, not having enough money for our needs, paying the bills, having children, having healthy children, raising children who turn out well, homeschooling, paperwork, business decisions, my health, college decisions, and so on.

Fear had stolen so much from me. *No more!* I wish I could have the times back when I was homeschooling my kids and was only partly there because my worries were swirling around in my mind. I would have laughed and enjoyed the time so much more. Thankfully, we don't have to live in fear. As the Bible says, **"There is no fear in love; but perfect love casts out fear, because fear involves punishment, and the one who fears is not perfected in love" (1 John 4:18).**

God is love. He can cast out all fear. He commands us not to fear anyone or anything except for Him, and He tells us to give Him all of our burdens and concerns. The Bible says, **"Be anxious for nothing, but in everything by prayer and supplication with thanksgiving let your requests be made known to God. And the peace of God, which surpasses all comprehension, will guard your hearts and your minds in Christ Jesus" (Philippians 4:6,7).** What a wonderful promise! We can pray and ask God to take care of all our needs, and in exchange we can have His peace.

We have to *choose* not to be anxious and not to allow fear to steal our joy. I am still tempted, quite often, to give in to fear. Now, I choose to take my thoughts captive and proclaim God's truths over my life. I recite scripture verses which hold God's promises for me and for my life. The great news is that all of His promises hold true for you, too! We can take control of our thoughts with God's help, and replace our thoughts with His.

I believed that God told me he would heal my heart "soon." How soon is soon in God's time? I had people at church pray for my healing; my husband fasted and prayed for an entire week. Over the next three years, I had prayer from different people at different times. I was tempted to doubt but continued to speak words of healing over myself. One day, I realized I had forgotten to take my medication for two days. My heart felt great, better than ever. A trip to the cardiologist confirmed all was well, and I could be off all medication. Praise God!!

I still have moments when I feel my heart skip a beat or give a flutter. When that happens, fear is knocking at my door. I proclaim that I am healed by Jesus Christ and that in Him I have no reason to be afraid. I know that being anxious can be a temptation for me, but I have given it over to the Lord. Sometimes it is moment by moment, but I want to live in His freedom and joy. My God can move mountains; He has cattle on one thousand hills; He can raise the dead and create life! When I remind myself of His power, His might, and His great love, peace floods my heart and all fear is gone.

As wives and mothers, we need to guard against the fear of man, in terms of what others think of us. Our guide throughout life is God, who provides a wonderfully practical manual in His Word, the Bible. The enemy loves to tempt us to try to please others or look good to them, sometimes to the detriment of ourselves and our families. The Bible says, **"The fear of man brings a snare, but he who trusts in the Lord will be exalted" (Proverbs 29: 25).** Studying God's Word and spending time in His presence is vital to our fruitfulness, joy, and peace. When we know who God is and what He thinks of us, we can focus on what will please Him and on what is His best for us.

Real Life Counts!

I remember being asked quite a few times after month-long trips to both France and New Zealand, "Did you *do school*?" My husband and I would inwardly chuckle as we thought about our family learning some French language and culture, skiing in the Alps, converting kilometers and grams to miles and pounds, seeing castles, observing the world's only land colony of albatross, exchanging currency, boating through fjords, walking up to glaciers, viewing new wildlife, and meeting other homeschool families. Outwardly we would answer politely that we had all learned a great deal; however, we had left our math books at home.

Trips like these have been wonderful opportunities for adventure and learning, and it has been easy for us to realize the educational and spiritual value they have had in our lives. But what about the everyday? What about the tedious and repetitive, the interruptions to our schedules whether unpleasant or welcomed?

We live on a farm in Pennsylvania where we have a butcher shop and cheese making facility. On our farm we have cows, pigs, chickens, and horses. Once in a while something escaped and we needed to drop our schoolwork and have a round-up. Personally, I always enjoyed these spontaneous rodeos as a way to get a little exercise and fresh air and to break up the day. Plus, it was just plain fun! Afterwards, everyone was ready to focus again on schoolwork. Other interruptions may not have been as pleasant or as timely: the USDA inspector needed me to make immediate changes on our written plans, an employee needed to be taken to get stitches, a couple of the kids were needed for an urgent farm task, someone dropped by and needed to talk, or a child was sick and needed to go to the doctor. The list of interruptions is endless, and we can each fill in numerous other examples.

I used to get extremely stressed out if something or someone interrupted our homeschool day. As each year passed, the Lord worked on me, and I became more relaxed and more accepting of these "interruptions" as I began to see God's hand in them. God is sovereign and allows people and events into our lives to help mold and shape us into His image. Recognizing that God permits these "interruptions" to punctuate my life has allowed me to be more accepting and to be on the lookout for ways to glorify Him.

The year we started our cheese-making was a perfect example. We hired a consultant who guided my husband through the construction of our cheese-making room. Not only did we need a sanitary room with special wall-coatings, but we required a host of specialized equipment and various permits and inspections. When everything was in order and ready, our consultant flew out to our farm and lived with us for the week while he taught us to make cheese. All of us were on "cheese patrol" that week, as the learning curve was steep. We needed to cut cheese cloths, help make cheese forms, empty gallons of whey into barrels, calibrate pH meters, and more. Our school that week was cheese! In addition to learning about all things cheese, we learned many problem-solving techniques.

When we took our month-long trips, I learned to document our learning so that I could later present it in our portfolios in a way that reflected the true learning that had taken place. When we listened to books on tape, that was documented as literature. Map reading and navigating were recorded as geography, hiking or skiing was physical education, and so on. When I looked down our list at the end of the month even I was impressed! We truly had learned and experienced many new and wonderful things.

Are you attending a concert or a play? That can be documented for your child's portfolio as music or drama or fine arts. Field trips can be listed as science or history. Caring for older relatives or making meals for a needy family might be listed under home economics or service.

I am not advocating the rejection of more disciplined studies. We still worked on math skills, reading, writing, history, science, and Bible; however, life's unexpected interruptions often presented us with some of our most memorable learning opportunities. **Proverbs 16:9 says, "The mind of man plans his way, but the Lord directs his steps."** When circumstances are not what you expect, or what you desire, remember that God's hand is still in them.

God is the perfect father, the ultimate teacher. He has an individualized lesson plan for each one of us. In any given set of circumstances, He can be teaching each family member something completely different, something He knows each person needs to learn to grow closer to Him. What a comforting thought! We can trust God to teach us all we need to know as parents and disciples, and we can trust Him to teach our children as well.

Tips for Real Life Learning:

- Document it for what it is.
- Trust that God has a plan and purpose in all things.
- Embrace your family's unique situation/opportunities.
- Relax and be thankful in the moment.
- Looking back, see all you accomplished.

CHAPTER 4

Practical Ideas

A S I THINK back over all our years of homeschooling, there are quite a few helpful tips that come to mind. Hopefully these will give you some practical ideas to make your homeschool days more enjoyable and fruitful. These suggestions are in no particular order; they may spark some new ideas of your own. Enjoy!

Focus on character and spiritual training. At the end of your homeschool years, when your children are ready to leave home, what do you want for them? For us, our biggest goal was that they would accept Jesus Christ as Lord and Savior and have a lifestyle of continually seeking and serving God. Reading the Bible daily is a huge part of training up your children in the Lord. Read the Bible, memorize scripture, and discuss what you read. Take time to work on character issues; stop math if there is some situation you need to address. This is the hardest and most constant part of homeschooling, but the stakes are huge! The time and sacrifices you make will be well worth it!

Teach your children to serve others. Make meals for a sick friend, visit an older person, weed the yard for Grandma, or make food bags to give to homeless people. The lists are endless. My husband occasionally took our children to Philadelphia to give coffee to the homeless. We served meals to victims of the Delaware River flood and helped elderly relatives with grocery shopping, laundry, and household chores. Teach your children early to serve others so it becomes part of their lifestyle.

Listen to audio books while in the car. We used to get books from the library and listen to them on the way to the grocery store or while running errands. Together we enjoyed some wonderful literature, learned Bible verses to music, and made good use of our travel time. An added plus was that the kids rarely argued while captured by a wonderful story!

The grocery store can provide useful lessons. When the kids were small, I made them each a picture list with a little drawing for each item (maybe only 3 items per child). As we went through the store, they were responsible to find their items so we could put them in our shopping cart. This made them feel important and gave them something to focus on during the trip. As they got older, we sometimes used pages from a book called Grocery Cart Math, by Jaye Hansen, which provided interesting math activities to complete that were related to grocery shopping (comparing prices of generic vs brand names, calculating unit pricing, etc.).

Don't stress over life's "interruptions." Sometimes you have a particularly busy or stressful season, an illness, or some family event that takes more time out of your days and makes your usual homeschool routine difficult or impossible. Trust God and don't fret. Some of these interruptions can be the most valuable learning experiences of all. When we were in the middle of our busy deer processing season and needed our kids to help, we just focused on Bible, language, and math, and put science, history, and other subjects on hold for a little while. Our kids learned many real-life skills during this time, plus they learned to work together as a family.

Sometimes you may just need to take a break, for your own sanity or for that of your kids! You may want to try a short unit study or capitalize on the interest of a child. I remember one time when our son became fascinated with some animals that natives reportedly had seen in the rain forest, and he spent a week researching and writing all about his discoveries. Remember that learning is a part of life, not just reserved for designated "school" time.

Document real life learning. Is there a great field trip opportunity? Don't pass it up because you feel tied to your curriculum. Do you have a chance to visit a local business or take a factory tour? Take advantage of life's spontaneous moments, then document the learning that took place. If you listen to an audio book on your way, that can be documented as literature. Have your kids help you read a map for geography study. After your trip, your kids can record their thoughts or notes in a journal or illustrate the trip for an art project.

Take pictures. Whenever you do an interesting activity or take a field trip, document it with pictures. You can print these out to put in your portfolio. It's amazing how many things you forget as the year progresses, and pictures help you remember.

Let your children spend lots of time outdoors. Our children spent time on the swing set, in the hammock, making pretend American Indian villages, playing in the sandbox, taking nature walks, and more. If your kids play outside, they will get exercise and fresh air and sunlight; they will use their imaginations and their bodies to run, play, and laugh. When they are outside, they will not be focused on the computer, cell phone, TV, or other technology (make sure they leave electronics inside!).

Have your kids write notes and letters as part of writing instruction. They can make Grandma and Grandpa a sweet card, send thank you notes for birthday or Christmas gifts, or write a letter to a child in another country. Use real-life writing opportunities whenever possible.

Let your kids learn to write checks and pay bills. From a young age, have your children learn these skills while doing them with you. My kids felt so important sitting at my desk and writing, in PEN, on checks. They learned how much the electricity and phone bills cost and how to address letters. You can help them learn how to pay bills on-line, a skill they will most certainly need. They can learn to reconcile a checking account. When they are old enough, let them get an account of their own and help them learn to manage it. You will set them up for a successful future in managing their finances well.

Teach as many subjects as you can to your children collectively. If possible, teach your kids Bible, history, and science together. Plan field trips the whole family will enjoy. The more you can combine subjects, the less stressful planning will be. Of course, if your children are far apart in age or if you have many children, this will be more difficult. You may still be able to group several children together for some subjects. Language and math can be individualized, but it is helpful to group other subjects together when possible.

Keep up with current events. We used to get a subscription to a Christian student newspaper. Our kids would spend some time each week reading the current events articles. Sometimes they wrote summaries or made "newscasts" about topics of interest. You can make a video recording of your newscast and share it with Dad after dinner for a fun way to include him in your school day!

Give your kids chores to do. Chores help them become responsible and allow them to feel they are truly contributing to the family. By faithfully completing chores, your children will learn how to work hard, manage their own time, and value free time.

Kids can do a lot more than we give them credit for! Even at two years old, a child can be taught to make a bed. It may not look perfect, but it's good practice. Young children can take out the trash, vacuum, empty the dishwasher, sweep, and help you prepare meals. They love to do grown up jobs. Training your children in chore completion can take extra time, but it pays off in the long run. When your kids are a little older, you will find you have a wonderfully helpful little team to help keep your household running smoothly.

We also had many jobs around the farm and in our butcher shop for our kids to help us with. One son invented a K'NEX machine to do his "boring" job of rolling up labels for us! Contributing to the family in real and tangible ways builds family unity, as well as confidence and useful skills.

Let your kids help you with "real" jobs. From a young age, kids love to help. A two-year-old can hold and hand you tools, help put groceries away, and feed your pets. Let your children watch Dad change the oil in the car; if he does it often enough over the years, he will learn how to do it completely by himself. So many important life skills can be taught this way. Your children will develop confidence and maturity as they become more skilled and capable. When possible, let your kids help you. Include them in all aspects of your life so that your family becomes a team working together.

It's okay for your kids to have some free time when they feel bored! One of the unexpected gifts of homeschooling and having more time is the freedom for your kids to feel bored. If they cannot turn on the TV or play computer games, they will find ways to become creative and may discover new hobbies or interests. Our kids built teepees, played with Playmobil toys outside, made forts, cracked open acorns, played with Legos, remounted a go-cart engine onto a trash-picked mini bike, wrote plays to perform for family and friends, and took apart an old chainsaw and put it back together so that it worked. Allow your kids the freedom to explore. You never know what gifts they may discover!

If kids seem restless or unfocused, let them do chores or physical exercise before schoolwork. Most children, and boys especially, seem to benefit from doing chores, running a few laps around the house, or doing yardwork prior to focusing on schoolwork. Pay attention to your kids and make your schedule fit the personalities and learning styles of your particular children. A little physical exercise first can make your school time more focused and fruitful.

Adjust your schedule to fit your life. During our busy seasons, we completed our Bible reading together as a family and the children completed language and math independently. Science, history and other topics were put on hold as we did more "real life" learning and working together. You can do schoolwork on the weekends and take a weekday off. Give yourself permission to deviate from the schedule or to take a break. Interruptions and illnesses are part of life. Sometimes incredible field trips or educational moments present themselves. Go with it! Seek God as you plan your days and be open to His leading. Then, don't stress if you must adjust from time to time.

Use plenty of hands-on activities to learn about science and history. We loved the *Science in a Nutshell* kits by Delta Education. They provided excellent and simple activity guides and supplies for topics such as gears, electricity, crystals, levers, animals, etc. The planning was easy and the activities were so much fun. We went on nature walks and bike rides, taking our sketchpads and watercolors along to document discoveries or paint the scenery. Our son found an owl pellet in the woods, so we dissected it and laid out all the parts. Utilizing a microscope, creating chemical reactions, counting out change with real coins, building mini pyramids, and making cardboard castles all provided fun hands-on learning opportunities. Be creative and allow your children this freedom as well. The hands-on activities and field trips are the experiences my children remember most fondly.

Choose literature purposefully. Select books to help your children think and grow in maturity and faith. We liked to select books we thought would benefit our children; each child had his own shelf to choose from. On the shelf, we placed our top choices for them. Our kids liked having a narrower selection to choose from, rather than the whole library. Of course, they could always select something else if they desired, but they generally stuck to the pile from their shelf. In addition to fiction, historical fiction, and Christian biographies, we chose books on finding a godly spouse, running a Christian business, learning to take your thoughts captive, etc. Make the most of the time your children are at home, and decide which books you want them to learn from before they leave. Also, if you really want them to hear a book, read it aloud- everyone loves to be read to!

Read aloud daily. Reading aloud increases a child's attention span and exposes him to vocabulary and content well above his reading level. Plus, it provides togetherness, laughter, and snuggle time! I recall several times when we were reading a great book (*The Hiding Place* by Corrie Tenboom and *The Golden Goblet* by Eloise Jarvis McGraw) aloud in the car, and we stayed in the car after arriving home so we could finish the book and see what happened. I read aloud to our children all the way through high school, and those were such fun times. Often, the children would make comments during our reading time that made us all laugh to the point of tears. Those times of sharing and laughter are now among my most favorite memories.

Get involved in the community. For us 4-H was an amazing opportunity to meet other families who enjoyed agricultural activities. We all made life-long friends and had opportunities to connect with people from many different walks of life. If your children are musical or love drama, they can join a community orchestra or drama group. Are they athletic? Community sports are a great way to meet others outside your traditional homeschool or church circles.

Plan your meals a week at a time. Fold a piece of paper in half lengthwise. On the left hand side list 5 to 7 meals for the week, including where to find the recipes (i.e. Church cookbook p. 10). On the right hand side list any ingredients you need to purchase. After you do this for all recipes, you can cut the paper in half and hang the menu on the refrigerator and take the shopping list with you to the store. Be sure to plan in a night for leftovers if you have them. I liked having a list because I could look at the beginning of our school day and pick which recipe to make for dinner, thaw out meat if needed, and know I had all the ingredients required. Also, it helped me try out new recipes. The planning only took about 15 minutes and made the week much easier.

<u>Maintain planners and portfolios</u>. In Pennsylvania, homeschoolers are required to keep lesson plans documenting either 180 days of school or 900 hours. We have always documented days. I kept a one-page calendar where I highlighted every day we encountered a learning experience, either formal or informal. This helped me see when we had our 180 days completed. I counted field trips, travel, and real-life experiences. For each child, I also made a planner on the computer in which I wrote in each subject for each day and left room for notes. The child could then check off each box as completed. In the early days, I purchased planners which worked well for a while; however, I grew tired of writing in the subjects each day for all three children. By typing each child's individual planner on the computer, I saved myself recording time.

Portfolios containing samples of work in each subject area are also required in Pennsylvania. In my desk, I have a drawer which holds hanging file folders. Each child had a folder in the drawer into which we placed any tests, writing, photographs, or brochures that were "portfolio-worthy." Towards the end of the year, we made scrapbook pages out of the photographs and slipped the written work and scrapbook pages into sheet protectors, which were all placed in a three-ring binder that served as our portfolio. We still love to look through these portfolios, which chronicle each year in photos, field trips, compositions, and other work. All thirteen years of portfolios for each child were on display at their graduation parties; a precious way of presenting a snapshot of their lives up until that point.

<u>Plan field trips</u>. Every summer, a good friend and I sat down with our calendars and a list of ideas and planned one field trip for each month. We tailored the trips to the ages of our children and, whenever possible, coordinated with topics we were studying. Participating with another family made the trips extra special for the children as well as the parents. After the field trips, we usually had the kids write, illustrate, or journal about what they saw and learned. Some of our all-time favorite memories are the trips we took with our dear friends!

<u>Plan mini co-ops with like-minded families</u>. We only did this for a couple of years, but it worked well for us. Two other moms and I set up an every-other-week afternoon co-op in which each mom taught either art, music or health/physical education. This was a great way to add some extra fun and interest to our weeks. Both moms and kids enjoyed the social aspect as well as the creativity inspired by meeting with other families. Because there were only three families involved, the planning was simple, and we could adjust the schedule easily if needed.

<u>When children are small, use playpen or room time.</u> If you allow children to spend small amounts of time in a safe and quiet space with a few selected educational toys, they learn to focus and develop a longer attention span. I found this so helpful when I had an infant who was getting up in the night because I could rest while my older child was quietly playing in a playpen or his room.

<u>Limit computer time.</u> We made a chart with squares which represented 20 minute blocks of time to use for fun educational games. Our kids were allowed to check off six blocks per week and we used a small timer which was kept right next to the computer. Put your computer in a prominent place in the house and monitor its use.

<u>Set up rules if your older children have cell phones</u>. We had a rule that there were no phones allowed in the bedroom, at meals, or during school time. Just like the computer, we need to be careful about what we allow into our homes via electronic devices.

<u>Keep a shelf or plastic tub for each child's materials.</u> It is helpful for each child to have a specific place to keep his own materials. We used sturdy plastic tubs with flip-up lids, which served us well for many years. Each child kept planners, math books, notebooks, and supplies in the tub, while items everyone used were kept separately. This made it easy to find things and get started each day without having to search around the house for materials. When schoolwork was completed for the day, materials went back in the tubs and could be stashed out of the way.

Tie language into other studies. When possible, tie your literature and writing into what you are learning in history, Bible, and science. This is a great way to practice writing skills and reinforce learning in other areas. We especially liked the *Institute for Excellence in Writing* materials, as they are designed for this very purpose.

Find some special ways to celebrate your children's accomplishments. At the end of each school year, we held an open house where we displayed the children's portfolios. We invited grandparents and a few dear friends and made a lovely dessert buffet. This was a fun way to show what we had done and to celebrate each of our children. Grandparents loved sitting with them and looking at their schoolwork and pictures, which represented the hard work and activities of the year.

When each child graduated, we had a big graduation party. I made up a slide show for each child and displayed portfolios from grades K-12. We had a huge buffet, a beautiful cake, and decorations. My husband started off the meal by offering a special prayer of thanksgiving and blessing for the graduate. These were extremely meaningful and memorable events for us as a family.

Use the high school years to customize learning. If your child already anticipates future career goals or has plans for college, you can customize these years to prepare. Does he plan to go to college? He can take community college or on-line courses which count twice, once for high school and once for college credit. Is he planning to start into the work force? He can job shadow or try different apprenticeships. Don't give all your kids the same generic education. By the high school years, gifts and interests start to show. Let God give you guidance for each child and design a curriculum to fit.

In the high school years, take CLEP exams when possible. CLEP stands for College Level Examination Program. When passed, these exams earn college credits. The tests usually last less than ninety minutes and cost less than one hundred dollars. The student either passes or fails. A passing score can translate into three or more college credits, which can be transferred to a college of your choice. After completing a rigorous course, such as chemistry, biology, physics, or Algebra II, it is a great idea to purchase a CLEP study guide and spend a couple of extra weeks studying for the exam. You can sign up for it at any time and community colleges usually have convenient testing times available. Both of our sons studied for and passed CLEP exams. These save time and money!

Carve out one-on-one time with each child. When younger children are napping, do something special with the oldest. Take one child alone with you on errands. Go fishing, take a bike ride, play a game, read a book, or take a walk. It doesn't need to be expensive or fancy. This individual time does great things for your relationships and makes each child feel special. We had our children keep lists of their favorite ideas for "special times." As they grew older, their lists changed. My husband took our sons on hunting trips, and my daughter and I shared "Girls' Weeks" at home, or took our own fun getaways. We still make an effort to plan special trips and activities with our children. These continue to be memorable and relationship-building times.

Get ideas from others but don't compare. Talk to other moms, read books, attend conferences and learn all you can about how to best homeschool your kids. Pray about it, then step out in faith, but don't compare! Remember, your family is unique, and God will show you what is best for you and your children.

CHAPTER 5

Day by Day; Year by Year

BACK IN COLLEGE, when I completed my student teaching, I sat in on different classes during my free periods to observe. Watching different teachers in action, I learned so much. Often, I picked up little tips on effective classroom management or discipline, positive ways to make learning exciting and engaging, new ways to organize recordkeeping, and sometimes I learned of things I would never do because they were ineffective. Whether the teacher was good, great, mediocre, or terrible, there was something to learn.

Real life practical examples are always helpful. They can give you tools to use right away or stir up new ideas of your own. This is my purpose in summarizing year by year what our school days looked like. Was it perfect? No! Would I do things exactly the same way again? Probably not. We all learn and grow along the way doing the best we can with what we know. In general, I am pleased with the way most of our days and years unfolded. My hope and prayer is you will gain a picture of what our days looked like, an idea of the materials we found useful, and some tools or ideas to help you as you continue your homeschool journey.

(One note here: This chapter mentions numerous resources which we utilized. Some we enjoyed more than others. Our favorite resources, the books and materials we found most helpful, are described in more detail in chapter 7.)

First Year of Homeschooling (Ages 5, 4, 2)

Our first year we journeyed to our attic for "school," which lasted no more than an hour or two. We read the Bible together and had a felt board that we used to illustrate the Bible stories. We desired to bring God's Word into the hearts of our children at an early age. In these early years, children soak up information and can easily memorize, so it is a great time to recite Bible verses. We just repeated our verse or passage out loud together each day until it was memorized. After Bible time, we prayed together.

I read other books out loud, and the children completed simple math workbook pages and worked on letters and basic phonics. My two-year-old played while the older two completed any written work. The kids each had a journal in which they wrote from time to time. Of course, they could not yet read, so it was just a bunch of letters and spaces across the page. After they "wrote" they would tell me what it said and I would record their words below what they had written. Sometimes, my husband, a grandparent, or I would write a response back to them in their journals.

We enjoyed using a book called *Five in a Row*, by Jane Lambert, which had interesting lessons based on particular books. I recall one book we read which talked about all the starch going out of an individual. We took some spray starch and our iron and made a piece of clothing good and stiff. Then we sprayed water on the clothing and felt it grow limp. This was a fun way to learn a new vocabulary word. *Five in a Row* had numerous lessons like this and covered various topics in history, language, and science.

One little project we made was a book on the days of creation. We read the account of creation in Genesis. Each day, the kids would illustrate a day of creation and write the number of the day in their book. When the book was complete we bound it and made a library card for the back. Friends and grandparents who read it signed their names on the little card. This made our kids feel as if they had made something important and special.

After school time, the kids completed chores. Before breakfast they completed "room chores" which included quiet time, brushing teeth, getting dressed and making their beds. From an early age they emptied the dishwasher, took out trash, vacuumed, and did other household and farm chores. When chores were complete, they had free time to play. This basic schedule of time with God, school time, chores, then free time continued throughout our school years.

Second Year of Homeschooling (Ages 6, 5, 3)

Our schedule was similar to the previous year. Here is a sample of what a daily schedule and plan looked like for our family:

Bible: Memory verses and reading aloud.

History: Listened to biographies on CD: Wright Brothers, Booker T. Washington, Charles Lindberg, Thomas Edison, Abraham Lincoln, Harriet Tubman, Alexander Graham Bell.

Language: Used Bible verses as copy work (Charlotte Mason approach, see *The Well-Trained Mind* by Susan Wise Bauer) to practice handwriting and model effective sentence structure.

Read aloud many books (from the library and home). We enjoyed *Mrs. Piggle Wiggle* series by Betty MacDonald, *Harold and the Purple Crayon* by Crockett Johnson), and *The Little House on the Prairie* series by Laura Ingalls Wilder.

Reading Instruction: Abeka materials, *Teach your Child to Read in 100 Easy Lessons* by Siegfried Engelmann), *Phonics Pathways* by Dolores Hiskes.

Worked on *Doodle Loops* by Sandy Baker. Each exercise in the workbook had several simple sentences. The children had to read sentences and illustrate descriptions. This was a fun way for them to practice reading.

Math: Used simple workbooks, manipulatives.

Field Trips: Longwood Gardens, the zoo, an apple orchard, a tannery, Franklin Institute, Butterfly World, Sea World, a forestry operation in Florida, Silver Springs, a marine rescue center, nature walks, a helicopter museum, Howell Farm (old fashioned farm-hand shearing sheep, carding wool, etc.).

Third Year of Homeschooling (Ages 7, 6, 4)

By our third year, our family decided that we preferred to spend our time in our living room rather than in our attic. Most of our homeschool days were spent downstairs in our living room, dining room, or kitchen. Our attic became more of a school supplies storage area and playroom.

We started each day with our Bible time. After Bible and prayer, we completed history and science together. Instead of textbooks (until high school), we used literature and biographies as our reading material. I read aloud daily to the children for both history and science, and we completed experiments, projects, and activities together. Reading, language, and math lessons were individualized for each child. This basic format continued until our oldest was in junior high school. Even then we read the Bible and some history together.

Bible: Used felt pieces, read aloud, memorized verses and the books of the Bible, prayed together.

Service project: Packed seeds for Russia with Josh McDowell Ministries.

History/Language: Used Sonlight curriculum (literature-based approach).

Studied Genesis, Exodus, ancient Egypt, ancient Rome, the Vikings, medieval times.

Worked on spelling using a simple workbook and dictation exercises provided by Sonlight. Used a handwriting book, and *Explode the Code* by Nancy Hall for phonics. *Explode the Code* was especially helpful for my children early on when the physical act of writing was difficult. The text requires minimal writing and sometimes the children just need to put an "X" on the correct word. I loved these books for basic phonics practice.

Math: After trying several other publishers, we settled on *Saxon*. I loved how they incorporated manipulatives in the instruction for grades one through three. Also, upon switching, my oldest said, "Finally, a math book with no pictures to distract me." And to think I avoided it because I thought it appeared too boring with its black and white workbook pages!

Science: Used materials recommended by Sonlight. Topics included: water, weather, plants, fossils, space, electricity, magnets, dinosaurs, planets, food and nutrition, animals, and more. Read aloud and completed simple experiments and activities. Wrote up or illustrated simple lab sheets describing: what we used, what we did, what happened, and what we learned.

Field Trips/ Projects: Tapped Maple trees and made syrup, harvested honey, constructed a castle out of paper towel tubes and cardboard, made a model of Egypt and the Nile River, attended the Nutcracker, made our own coat of arms, wrote our names in hieroglyphics, and visited an archeology museum, the Hopewell Furnace, an insectarium, the zoo, Hawk Mountain, and a sheep shearing demonstration.

Co-Op: Participated in art, physical education and health, and music with two other families. Each mom taught one of the subjects and we met every other week. All of us enjoyed the social aspect of meeting together as we participated in fun activities, which supplemented our curriculum.

Fourth Year of Homeschooling (Ages 8, 7, 5)

Bible: Read Joshua, Ruth, I Samuel, II Samuel, I Kings, Psalms, Proverbs, learned memory verses, prayed together.

History/Language: Used *Beautiful Feet* curriculum, a literature-based approach by Rea Berg for early American history. Read books on Columbus, Pocahontas, Pilgrims, and some historical fiction such as *Johhny Tremain* by Esther Forbes. After reading, kids illustrated a scene from our reading and wrote a small caption underneath. Different activities are suggested in the slim and easy-to-use teacher's guide.

Over the years we used many of the *Beautiful Feet* study guides. They are concise and straightforward but provide excellent literature and activities to make learning memorable and fun. So many teacher's manuals can be wordy and overwhelming. My theory on teaching manuals was they had to be simple and easy to use; if I was overwhelmed by them I wouldn't want to use them. So, I chose carefully. These were some of my favorites!

Reading/Language: *Spelling Workout* by Modern Curriculum Press, *Writing Strands* by Dave Marks, Abeka language materials, *Write Away* by Great Source, *Happy Phonics* game by Diane Hopkins, and Zaner-Bloser Handwriting.

Each child read books quietly for a sustained amount of time. I had them set a timer to keep track of this. As they grew older and more skilled in their reading, the length of time increased. Of course, sometimes they wanted to read longer if they were in a particularly exciting part of the book! Using a timer was a great way to be sure they met a minimum amount of independent reading time. Our kids loved this time and they could often be found snuggled under a comforter stretched out on the couch, swinging gently outside in the hammock, or curling up on the floor with a kitten as they read their books. They kept a list of books completed in the back of their planners. Then, at the end of the year, we had a complete list of titles and authors for our portfolios. Every year from this year forward, the children spent time reading independently and maintained a book list. Although I did not record it here in each of the following year's outlines, independent reading was always a part of their language studies.

Math: *Saxon* textbooks for each grade, *Miquon Math* (manipulatives-based program published by Key Curriculum Press).

Science: *Science and the Bible* by Donald DeYoung, *Greg's Microscope* by Millicent Selsam, activities with a microscope, homemade experiments with "Mystery Powders" using the scientific method, *Green Thumbs: Radishes* by TOPS Learning Systems (grew radishes from seeds, documented growth, and made graphs).

Field Trips/ Projects: Plymouth Plantation and Mayflower II tour, Corning Glass Museum and camping trip with another family, Valley Forge, Pennsbury Manor (home of William Penn), art museum, science museums, local tile museum, Grounds for Sculpture (campus full of art sculptures and paintings), the zoo, skiing, box-making factory tour, Byer's Choice (factory where they make Christmas Caroler figurines), and a regional airport tour.

Co-Op (Art/Physical Education/Music): Worked on assorted art projects, completed the Presidential Fitness Test, participated in a homeschool gym class at the local Christian college, learned about the great composers and the orchestra.

As previously noted, we did our schoolwork Tuesday through Saturday and then had Sunday and Monday off as a family. Because our shop is open on Saturday, which is our busiest day, we have Monday off. Homeschooling allowed us this flexible schedule and the ability to still enjoy a two-day family weekend. Mondays were great days for special trips; much less crowded than Saturdays!

Standardized Testing: In Pennsylvania, standardized tests are required in grades 3, 5, and 8. We were able to sign up for these through a local group of homeschoolers. Many different tests are accepted by the state and there is no minimum test score requirement. Our kids needed to take the tests and show the results to our evaluator. Aside from these tests and the SAT's, there were no other standardized tests we required our kids take over the years. Some families choose to take tests yearly to give their kids practice in the skill of test-taking and to see how their children's scores compare to other kids of the same age.

Fifth Year of Homeschooling (Ages 9, 8, 6)

Bible: Read, studied, narrated and discussed: Esther, Job, Jonah, Micah, Matthew, John, Acts, and Proverbs. Memorized and recited Bible verses.

History/Geography: *Beautiful Feet Geography.* We read *Paddle to the Sea, Seabird, and Minn of the Mississippi* by Holling Clancy Holling. With these books we followed a tiny carved canoe's journey from the Great Lakes to the Atlantic, traced Seabird's voyage on a world map, and recorded a turtle's travels down the Mississippi River. We toured Colonial Williamsburg, studied the colonial time-period, attended a colonial Christmas, read *The Witch of Blackbird Pond* by Elizabeth George Speare, studied the Quakers, and toured Pennsbury Manor (William Penn's home).

Utilized Audio-Memory materials to sing the states and capitals, continents and oceans, countries and regions of the world.

Language: Reading, grammar exercises, dictation, spelling, editing. Whenever possible, writing reinforced our studies in history, Bible, and science.

Math: *Saxon* textbooks, hands-on activities, real-life math applications when possible. One great book we found and used over the elementary years was *Grocery Cart Math* by Common Sense Press. Occasionally we chose one of the activities, and the kids brought along a clipboard and worksheet when we did our shopping. The activities provided a fun break from routine work while offering new insight into real-life uses of math.

Science: *Science in a Nutshell* kits by Delta Education. We explored crystals, gears, planets, space, earth science, snapping turtles, rocks and minerals, animals, reptiles, forestry, and manufacturing.

Field Trips/ Projects: Museum of Natural Science, multiple factory tours of meat processing equipment, cheese plant tour, Martin Guitar Factory tour, pretzel factory tour, Crystal Cave, NJ Science Museum, two zoos, a trout hatchery, honey harvesting, a nature preserve, Homosassa Springs, and Colonial Williamsburg.

Co-Op: Art, gym, and music every other week with two other families.

Business: My husband helped each of our children establish their own businesses. Our oldest son bottled and sold the honey we harvested; our daughter raised chickens and sold the eggs in our store; our youngest made cranberry relish for Thanksgiving and sold it in our store.

Sixth Year of Homeschooling (Ages 10, 9, 7)

Bible: Read aloud books of the Bible, prayed together, learned memory verses.

History: Studied US and world history using Hillyer's *A Child's History of the World*. Watched videos on Harriet Tubman, Christopher Columbus, George Washington, Abraham Lincoln, Louis Pasteur, and the Wright Brothers.

Language: Reading, grammar exercises, dictation, spelling, editing. Whenever possible, writing reinforced our studies in history, Bible, and science.

Materials: *Spelling Power* by Beverly Adams-Gordon, *Wordsmith Apprentice* by Janie Cheaney, *Institute for Excellence in Writing, Just Write* by Elsie Wilmerding and Alexandra Bigelow, and *A Reason for Handwriting* by Carol Ann Retzer and Eva Hoshino.

Spelling Power is a great book which can be used for every spelling level. The main concept in this text is to take a pretest and then study the words missed. The text provides a checklist of steps to follow to learn the words. A final test is given to be sure the targeted words have been mastered. The parent must give the pre-tests and post-tests.

Institute for Excellence in Writing: Writing Intensive is a set of instructional DVD's and materials. Lessons are interesting, funny, and age appropriate. I love how you can use these materials to systematically teach both the structure and style of writing. These techniques can be used as you have your children write about topics you are studying in other subject areas. You can also use the lessons for multiple ages and abilities.

Math: *Saxon* math materials.

Science: Flight (lift, air pressure, jets, helicopters, space travel, hot air balloons), electricity (electron paths, conductors, insulators, open/closed circuits, parallel/series circuits), videos on the blood, the sun, Louis Pasteur, Apollo 13 and rocketry, used a microscope, and went on nature walks.

Materials: *Science in a Nutshell Electrical Connections* Kit, and *Flight! Gliders to Jets* Kit by Delta Education.

Field Trips/ Projects: Played community soccer/football, skiing, snowmobiling, helped feed flood victims, built a go-cart with Dad, Herr's Potato Chip Factory tour, Kennedy Space Center, forestry operations tour, beekeeping and honey harvesting, Presidential Rally for George W. Bush, wrote checks to pay household bills, worked in butcher shop packaging meat, toured Greenfield Village (Henry Ford, Thomas Edison's lab).

Co-Op (Art, Music, Physical Education): Studied art history and sculpture, the lives and works of great composers, the circulatory and nervous systems, including dissection of a cow's heart and a deer brain.

Our older son started playing community football.

Seventh Year of Homeschooling (Ages 11, 10, 8)

Bible: We continued as in past years.

History: *History of Science* by Rebecca Manor. We studied great scientists from Archimedes up to Pasteur and completed an experiment for each scientist. We subscribed to a Christian news magazine to keep abreast of current events.

Language: We completed independent reading assignments for each child as well as individualized writing assignments.

Materials*: Institute for Excellence in Writing: Writing Intensive* by Andrew Pudewa, *Calvert Spelling* CD's (these are similar in set up to the techniques in *Spelling Power* but can be done independently on the computer), *Word a Week Vocabulary Program* by Ruth Foster, *English from the Roots Up* by Joegil Lundquist for the study of Greek and Latin roots of words.

Math: *Saxon* math materials, *Math Detective* by Terri Husted, and *Math Word Problems* by Anita Harnadek.

The older two children used a math CD-ROM that accompanied their textbooks. Lessons were presented and writing appeared on the screen as the instructor explained the math concepts. After listening to the lesson, the children completed math exercises, then checked their answers. If any answers were incorrect, they re-worked the problems until they were accurate. At this point, I stepped in to help only when needed. Because we corrected all the math problems which were incorrect, we did not give tests or quizzes up until the high school level when we had to provide grades and transcripts. Working for mastery rather than just "covering" a topic is one of the tremendous advantages of homeschooling.

With the older two independently working on their math lessons, I was free to teach our youngest his math lesson and help him with other subjects as well.

Science: *Real Science-4-Kids: Chemistry* by Rebecca Keller. This text provided a great, simple explanation of chemistry, complete with fun experiments and projects. We made our own litmus paper, formed molecules out of marshmallow, created slime, and more.

Field Trips/ Projects: Niagara Falls, service project in Camden feeding people for a children's benefit, Ellis Island, The Statue of Liberty, Philadelphia Zoo, tour of a vet's office, orchard, skiing, Museum of Archaeology, Asher Chocolate Factory, sewing projects, cross country skiing, tour of The Wall Street Journal, a writer's workshop with authors Dave and Neta Jackson, and a month's time living in France.

Let me elaborate on our trip to France for a moment here. A friend of ours owns a home in France on Lake Geneva, and he offered to let us stay there free of charge for the month. We bought our plane tickets, packed our bags and a cooler full of our meats, leased a minivan when we arrived, and embarked on our adventure.

During our time in France, we met up with another homeschool family with whom we connected through the HSLDA (Homes School Legal Defense Association) website. My husband suggested we try to meet other homeschoolers while in France, so I went on the HSLDA website and found an email link. I sent a brief email and had some responses. We met with one of these homeschool families and toured the Evian Water Plant together. We toured the Gruyere cheese plant, skied in the Alps many days, visited the Olympic Museum, toured a trout hatchery, ate escargot and fondue, visited cheese stores and butcher shops and local bakeries, learned about French grocery markets, and experienced what if feels like to be immersed in another culture and language.

This trip to France was the first time our children had flown in a plane, so all the details of travel, from passports and airports to the flight itself and customs officials, were new to them. The entire month was full of excitement and learning. What an incredible opportunity!

Art/Music/Physical Education: Sewing, glass making, singing at church, and community sports.

Eighth Year of Homeschooling (Ages 12, 11, 9)

This year of homeschooling became one of transition as our oldest entered his junior high school years. Instead of our Tuesday through Saturday school week, we adjusted to the typical Monday through Friday routine. Our oldest decided he wanted to play sports at the public school, and this new schedule would be a better fit.

For history, each child worked on a literature-based curriculum. This was the first year we did not study history all together. I worked with our youngest while the older two completed their assignments independently.

Bible, science, music, and art were still completed together, and we all sat together in our living room for most of the other subjects. Each child had his own planner and marked off assignments as completed. I moved from child to child, helping as needed. During this time, I could also switch a load of laundry, begin some food preparation, or complete other chores.

Bible: We read aloud books of the Bible, prayed together, and learned memory verses.

History: Our oldest completed a *Beautiful Feet* study on ancient history which included Egypt, Greece, and Rome. He read, wrote summaries, made illustrations and maps, recorded definitions, and completed projects to reinforce his learning.

Our daughter, who was fascinated with her pony, worked through the *Beautiful Feet* study entitled *The History of the Horse*. In addition to learning about anatomy and breeds of horses, she read classics such as *Black Beauty* by Anna Sewell and *Misty of Chincoteague* by Marguerite Henry.

I worked with our youngest and studied medieval times, knights, castles, and the Roman Empire. We purchased a mini knight kit, complete with a sword and armor. He drew pictures and wrote about what we learned. We used the *Usborne Book of World History* by Anne Millard, and *The Usborne Time Traveler* by Judy Hindley.

This year was a fun change for all of us. Much of our reading and writing reinforced our history studies. I always felt the kids learned so much more if we could connect the subjects rather than treat each one as if it was its own separate entity.

Language: Seventh grade was the first year we used a grammar book for our oldest. *Easy Grammar Plus* by Wanda Phillips, a big red book, was completed over the course of seventh and eighth grades. We followed this same pattern for the younger two children when they reached this age. We used Calvert spelling CD-ROMs on the computer, handwriting books, and our history study guides for writing topics.

Math: *Saxon* math materials.

This year, our oldest took a break from *Saxon* to spend some time on real-life math skills and to improve his basic arithmetic and algebra skills in preparation for higher math. In the seventh grade year, we let each child follow this same course. During this year, our son completed *Key to... Books*, by Steven Rasmussen, which focused on percent, fractions, decimals, and algebra. He wrote checks to pay household bills and completed other practical math activities. The younger two continued with *Saxon* math.

Science: We used *Science in a Nutshell* kits by Delta Education for magnets, static electricity, and geology. Our real-life experiences around the farm, in the butcher shop, and in our travels always taught us a huge amount about God's creation. We attempted to hatch wild turkey eggs (unsuccessfully), kept bees and harvested honey, cared for pet reptiles, made cheese, and traveled to New Zealand. Our daughter participated in a 4-H beef club where she raised and trained a cow to show at the local grange fair.

Field Trips/ Projects: San Diego Zoo, Franklin Institute, pottery workshop, wildflower preserve, aquarium, fund raiser for a local mission, CHEESE-MAKING, a trip to NEW ZEALAND.

During our trip to New Zealand, we met other homeschool families (we used our HSLDA connection once again), read maps, converted kilometers to miles, exchanged currency, toured cheese and venison plants, went possum hunting, saw glow worms, milked sheep, spun wool, sheared a sheep, hiked to a glacier, went on a nature cruise, witnessed bungee jumping, watched incredible wildlife, viewed breathtaking scenery, and learned about native plants and animals as we traveled the country in our rented motorhome. Wow! What an incredible three weeks of unforgettable learning!

Art: Origami, painting, clay sculpting, leaf pressing, knitting (our daughter made scarves for the homeless), and watercolors.

Music: Used an instructional music CD-ROM called *Music Ace* by Harmonic Vision, which taught note reading, pitch, tone, and other musical concepts. Studied the life and works of: Bach, Handel, Mozart, Beethoven, and Tchaikovsky. Studied the history and lyrics of our national anthem. Listened to geography songs to learn capitals, countries, and continents. Our daughter played Mary in the church Christmas musical.

I might add here that we are not an especially musically gifted family. In spite of this, we made sure to develop an appreciation and knowledge of music. Our daughter took violin lessons and our youngest learned the guitar. After a couple years of lessons, they stopped. The passion just wasn't there, nor was the gift.

Each family will have its own natural proclivities. While it is good to expose our children to many different experiences and activities, it is important to realize that they cannot excel at them all. As you move through life with your children, you will discover some of their talents and weaknesses, their likes and dislikes. All are good to know! God has given each of us talents and passions, and those are hints as to what we may choose as our vocation or as our service to Him. It is good to work on improving our weaknesses and those of our children; however, God has given us strengths and talents for us to use for His glory. One of our jobs as parents is to notice, point out, and affirm the gifts we see in our children. By acknowledging and encouraging them in their strengths, we can help them be who God has created them to be.

Physical Education: What our family lacked in music, we made up for in physical education. In addition to our active lifestyle of walking, running, biking, skiing, and other recreational sports, our kids played on community or school teams. Our daughter played soccer this year. Our youngest son played community basketball, and our oldest participated in football and wrestling at the local public school. Our daughter also spent time riding her pony.

Life Skills/Work: All of our children helped on the farm and in the business. This particular year, the older two spent time waiting on customers or taking phone orders. We had the children use an instructional computer CD-ROM (*Typing Instructor*) to learn how to type.

Ninth Year of Homeschooling (Ages 13, 12, 10)

Bible: Read aloud books of the Bible, prayed together, learned memory verses.

History: Studied the Middle Ages, Renaissance, and Reformation using *Story of the Middle Ages* by Michael McHugh and John Southworth, *Shakespeare Stories* by Leon Garfield, and *Favorite Medieval Tales* by Mary Pope Osborne.

Language: *Institute for Excellence in Writing, Easy Grammar, Calvert Spelling, Spelling Power*, read literature according to ability level and interest.

Each child had his own additional writing book. My oldest son used Apologia's *Jump-In*, my middle child worked in a book which involved reflection and journaling, and my youngest son used *Just Write* by Elise Wilmerding and Alexandra Bigelow.

Math: *Saxon* textbooks, hands-on activities, real-life math when possible. Our daughter had her 7th grade break from *Saxon* and worked on *Key to...* books along with practical math activities.

Science: Used *Exploring Creation with Zoology* (Apologia) for the basis of our studies on birds, bats, insects, and all flying creatures.

Field Trips/ Projects: Cheese-making, meat convention, PA Farm Show, brewery tour, Bastille Days festival (Milwaukee), grange fair (showing cattle and hogs), whale watching in Rhode Island, snowmobiling, Museum of Natural Science (Philadelphia), Washington D.C. (guided walking tour), Air and Space Museum, House of Representatives, US Senate, soap making, volcano and science center (Nicaragua), 4-H officer's training class, 4-H Beef Club (older 2 kids), 4-H Pig Club, Amish history in Lancaster.

Our daughter took her hunter's safety class (with me!). She participated in the 4-H Beef Club and served as secretary in the 4-H Pig Club.

Our older son served as secretary in the 4-H Beef Club and news reporter in the 4-H Pig Club. He also competed with the 4-H Shotgun Club. This year he decided he wanted to purchase a 4-wheeler, so he offered to skin deer to make the money he needed. Before school, he woke up very early and skinned deer. He then did his schoolwork, went to wrestling practice, ate dinner, and went back down to the deer cooler to skin more. He skinned 1,000 deer over the course of the season, purchased that 4-wheeler, and took excellent care of it!

Our younger son shot his first deer with Dad, learned to check in customers who brought deer in for processing, and cared for all of our pigs on the farm.

Mission Trip: We had the wonderful opportunity to take a mission trip to Nicaragua. We traveled with our family and two other individuals and connected with a missionary who permanently lived there. Our purpose was to help harvest wood out of the forest and set up a temporary saw mill to make boards, which would later be used to build houses and churches. The guys had machetes (our ten-year-old thought that was awesome! I prayed all fingers and toes would remain intact!) and worked in the forest to clear a road. After that was complete, my husband and another friend, who is a logger by trade, drove tractors through the forest to retrieve the targeted trees. They hauled the wood back to a portable saw mill where boards were made. My daughter and I provided cooking and water hauling. We had to walk about a quarter mile to a little stream, fill a five-gallon bucket with water, bring it back to our camp, treat it with bleach, then use it for cooking or doctor it up with powdered drink mix so we could drink it without it tasting like bleach. We spent time with the women and children, played kickball, and swam. It was eye-opening for all of us to see a third-world country. It made us especially thankful for the luxury of having delicious, clean running water with a touch of a handle at our kitchen sink!

Art: Worked on drawing techniques using *Drawing with Children* by Mona Brookes.

Music: Read *Great Christian Hymn Writers* by Jane Stuart Smith and Betty Carlson to learn the stories behind favorite hymns, continued working on the computer with *Music Ace.*

Physical Education: Our oldest played on the public school football and wrestling teams, and our youngest son played community football and basketball. Our middle child kept active with biking, running, swimming, and her usually active lifestyle.

As we look back over our years, condensed in this summarized form, it looks as if we did so many interesting things and took many amazing trips. We were blessed to have the time and opportunity for travel, and we are very thankful. However, we don't want you to look at this and in any way feel discouraged or as if you need to compare. My husband is a doer and a visionary. Many of our experiences are a result of our family following his lead in both business and personal endeavors. We did not homeschool perfectly; we are not perfect parents. We are Christians, just like you, trying to do our best to walk closely with our God and raise up a godly family to point others to Christ.

Plenty of our day to day routines were *routine.* We spent plenty of time doing chores, which were repetitive and tedious. During deer season, we sometimes felt as if all we did was work in the business with little time to do anything social. It was a ton of work and not always enjoyable. The hard times made us work at keeping our thoughts positive and thankful, rejoicing always and giving thanks, as we are reminded to do in **I Thessalonians 5:16-18.**

My purpose in showing you what we did is just to encourage you, provide ideas, or spark new thoughts. Please, do not for one moment feel what you do is any less important or exciting. God has given you a unique family with your own specific calling. Where you live, what you do, the church you attend, and the people you encounter are all your mission field and calling. Your job is to keep seeking the God who created you and draw near to Him. He will give you your assignments. Just keep your eyes open and learn to appreciate all of the little things around you. God is working in your life, and He has good plans for you and your family! Raising up your children to love and serve Him is your highest calling. Homeschooling allows you to do life with your family, an incredible gift! You can all learn and grow together, making mistakes and experiencing victories along the way. Be encouraged, but don't compare. God has a unique race only you can run; run it well!

Tenth Year of Homeschooling (Ages 14, 13, 11)

First Year of High School

Our goal, as our oldest son began high school, was to provide the best education possible, and to make it specific to our individual child. We wanted to prepare him for the future God was leading him towards. We realized for each child the high school years would look different; we also desired to leave as many doors open as possible until the Lord closed them. We made sure to provide each child with the required courses and credits for graduation and college, if it was what God desired. With this in mind, we enrolled in one of Pennsylvania's accredited diploma programs, the Mason Dixon Home School Association. We chose this option because of its flexibility, especially with the English requirement, and because it suited our family's lifestyle of learning, which included traditional study, apprenticeship, work, and hands-on projects.

In order to graduate with a high school education, the following courses were required:

English:4 credits (including literature, grammar, writing, and speech requirements)
Math:3 credits
Science:3 credits
Social Studies:3 credits
Arts and Humanities:2 credits.

Additionally, in grades 7-12 at least a half credit in each of the following was required: geography, civics, world history, US history, PA history, Algebra I and II, geometry, safety and fire safety, health and physiology, physical education, music, and art. We made sure each child received two years of study in a foreign language to fulfill any college requirements.

Now, to those of you who have not entered the high school years, this may seem overwhelming. It really does not have to be. Given the diploma program we used, a credit could be earned by any one of the following:

- 120 hours
- 120 logged entries
- Completing 2/3 of a textbook
- Writing a 10-page paper
- Taking a college course
- Taking a CLEP exam
- Another way approved by your homeschool evaluator
- Half credits were awarded by completing half of the above criteria

So, for example, since we are not a particularly musical or artistic family, we asked that our children keep a log of any music or art activities they completed over the course of grades 7-12. They recorded the date and activity. This could be as simple as attending a concert or making a craft. After the 60 logged entries were recorded, the half credit was complete. We simply checked it off the list and kept our log as documentation.

Civics was required, so we waited until our youngest son was in 7th grade (the other two children were in high school) and completed the work together, which fulfilled the requirement for all three kids at the same time. Geography, PA history, safety education, fire safety, and health were all covered little by little as a part of other studies. A simple log or checklist was all that was needed for documentation.

Physical education was easy for us because of all of the sports programs our kids participated in. We counted up the hours they were at practice or games and made sure it was over 120 (it was always well over). We did not keep an official log, but if anyone questioned us, we could easily add it all up and prove the required times were met.

For math and science, we usually completed 2/3 of a textbook. Notes, labs, quizzes or tests served as our documentation. For English and other subjects for which we read literature or used non-textbook materials, our planners showing the 120 days served as documentation. Our daughter completed two science credits in one year, just because she wanted to graduate early and attend nursing school.

Our older son received a credit for apprenticeship in meat science. He punched a time card when he worked in the butcher shop and we were able to document over 120 hours for the school year.

Your child can write a 10-page paper on a history topic and that could count as a history credit. He could spend 60 hours as an apprentice in a trade and earn a half credit for the year. Or, he could take a class at your community college, earning both high school and college credit simultaneously. The options and flexibility are what make homeschooling during the high school years so appealing. You can allow your children to try out different avenues of interest and help them discern God's path for them. Also, credits can be completed in more or less than one school year.

Many people throw in the towel of homeschooling during the junior and senior high school years. Let me encourage you to stick it out. This is the time to reap the rewards of the years of hard work! You only have a few more short years before your children will be grown and on their own. You have these precious years to talk with them, laugh with them, and learn and grow with them as they discover their gifts, talents, and passions.

Here are what our high school years looked like from a curricular perspective:

Bible: Read aloud books of the Bible, prayed together, learned memory verses.

History: We still did this all together. I read aloud and the kids did writing assignments, projects, map work, etc. We used Susan Bauer's *The*

Story of the World: Early Modern Times and Genevieve Foster's *Abraham Lincoln's World* and *George Washington's World* as our main texts. *Audio Memory Geography Songs* by Larry and Kathy Troxel provided us all with a fun way to memorize capitals, countries, and continents.

Language: Our high schooler utilized an individualized on-line writing tutor through *writeguide.com.* This website connected him with a tutor who helped him walk through the process of writing a ten-page paper on turkeys, his all-time favorite species to hunt. He completed *Daily Grams* by Wanda Phillips, which bolstered his grammar and editing skills. *Institute for Excellence in Writing* was utilized as he wrote about topics studied in history.

Our daughter also worked with the *Institute for Excellence in Writing* and the same on-line writing tutor who helped her write a fictional piece. She started her two-year course in *Easy Grammar,* working on an exercise each day. A Calvert spelling CD-ROM helped her improve spelling skills.

Our youngest used the following materials for language studies*: Institute for Excellence in Writing, Language Lessons for the Elementary Child* by Sandi Queen, *Italic Handwriting* by Barbara Getty & Inga Dubay, *Spelling Power* by Beverly Adams-Gordon, and a Calvert Spelling CD-ROM. He also used a *Beautiful Feet* study guide for the book *Tree in the Trail* by Holling C. Holling. The study guide provided writing and language activities along with geography and history studies.

All three children read literature that corresponded to history studies whenever possible.

Foreign Language: Our oldest used a homeschool computer version of *Rosetta Stone German.* The computer program maintained his scores and calculated his grade. It also served as a log for his 120 days.

Math: *Saxon* math materials with instructional computer CD.

Science: With the younger two children, we used Apologia's *Exploring Creation with Zoology 3: Land Animals*. We read together and completed many activities and experiments. Our field trip/vacation out west greatly added to our study of land animals.

Our oldest son used Apologia's Biology textbook by Dr. Jay Wile. He and another homeschooled friend completed the lab experiments together once a week.

Together, we dissected an owl pellet found in the woods, visited the Creation Museum, and attended an exhibit featuring the human body.

Field Trips/ Projects: 4-H Pig club for all three (my husband and I served as the leaders for eight years), 4-H Beef Club (older two children), *Typing Instructor* computer tutorial, Creation Museum (Kentucky), Grange Fair, peach orchard and packaging plant, community service (feeding the homeless and serving at a fundraiser for orphans), a trip to Florida, and a trip out west where we visited: Yellowstone National Park, the Badlands, Mt. Rushmore, and Custer State Park.

Art: Assorted projects and activities, our daughter sewed and practiced her photography.

Music: *Music Ace* (computer tutorial program) and *Great Christian Hymn Writers* (Smith and Carlson).

Physical Education: Community football for the youngest, junior high school field hockey for our daughter, and high school football and wrestling for our oldest.

Eleventh Year of Homeschooling (Ages 15, 14, 12)

Bible: Continued as in past years, reading together, praying, memorizing scripture.

History: What a blessing to still learn history all together. Bauer's *The Story of the World IV* along with accompanying outlines, maps, and activities served as our text. Our visits to two WWII museums and the Battleship New Jersey fit in perfectly with our modern world history studies.

Language: All of the children improved vocabulary with *Word a Week Vocabulary* (Teacher Created Resources). We also used David Quine's *Starting Points* (a literature based approach to developing a biblical worldview), which provided our oldest son with excellent literature and challenging writing assignments.

Our younger children improved spelling skills with Calvert's spelling CD-ROMs, and they continued refining grammar skills using *Easy Grammar Plus* (Phillips). They enjoyed *Story Starters* by Karen Andreola for writing prompts to compose some fictional pieces.

Our youngest child also utilized the following resources: *Editor in Chief* (Critical Thinking Books and Software), *Just Write Book 3* (Bigelow), Carol Ann Retzer's *A Reason for Handwriting* (he needed lots of handwriting practice), and *Institute for Excellence in Writing*.

Math: Our oldest son completed *Geometry* by Teaching Textbook and the younger two children worked on their *Saxon* math books. All three children calculated crop acreages and costs for their dad as a real-life math application.

Science: Our oldest son had the privilege of learning physics with his grandfather, a former high school physics teacher and aeronautical engineer. Each week they met together one day for several hours to cover the material for the week and complete experiments. Afterwards, we all ate lunch together. The very next year, my parents moved a long distance away. We were so thankful to have invested this time in a special relationship prior to this move. Physics instruction by an expert was just icing on the cake.

Our daughter counted her farm and 4-H activities for science time. We purchased Christian Light's *Home Economics* course, a series of workbooks which guided her through numerous activities on the topics of nutrition, meal preparation, child care, kitchen organization, etc. She planned and cooked meals for the family and canned pickles and peaches. I really enjoyed sharing this special course with my only daughter. She learned many of her homemaking skills from growing up on our farm and spending her days at home, but this course forced her to consider topics in much greater depth and detail. I felt especially blessed by our homeschooling lifestyle as I watched her grow into a young lady, now competent in running a household well.

We found some great hands-on science activities for our youngest son. He used *Lego Crazy Action Contraptions, Science in a Nutshell Kits* (electricity and gears), and *Snap Circuits* (electricity activities). Watching him work happily at the kitchen table on his various experiments and activities was a great joy.

Field Trips/ Projects: All of the children spent time with their dad hunting (deer, turkey, and geese). Over the years they have all had special hunting trips with him. My husband taught them a great deal about hunting, and they all have incredible memories of the special time spent together, enjoying God's creation with their dad.

All three kids participated in the 4-H Pig Club (our oldest son was elected as president and our daughter as news reporter) and the 4-H Shotgun Club. The older two children were members of the 4-H Beef Club, where our daughter served as Vice President. 4-H was an incredible blessing to our family. We met so many amazing families with similar values and work ethics. Many of the friendships we made continue to this day.

Other field trips this year included: a golf outing fundraiser for a ministry, the Omaha Zoo, two WWII museums, the American Association of Meat Processors convention, a 4-wheeler safety course, a hunter safety course, Florida (caverns, mangroves, Everglades), skiing, and snowmobiling in New Hampshire.

Foreign Language: Our oldest son completed a second year of German using the *Rosetta Stone* program.

Music: Our youngest son took guitar lessons for two years. Prior to this, our daughter completed one year of violin study. All the kids kept a log of their musical activities. We also continued reading about hymns and the stories behind them.

Physical Education: Community football for our youngest son, field hockey at the public school for our daughter, and football and wrestling at the public school for our oldest son.

Work/Apprenticeship: Our children all helped out in the butcher shop, waiting on customers over the holidays. They also helped with farm and house chores. Additionally, our oldest worked as an apprentice to his dad and logged close to 100 hours as he learned all about meat processing. He also took apart an old, broken chainsaw and got it working again. Over the years, we began to observe his mechanical gifting in many areas.

Our daughter faithfully cared for her chickens and helped, when needed, with retail in our store. The youngest salted all of our deer hides (around 1,000 of them) every deer season from this age until he left for college. He also made cranberry relish to sell in our store for Thanksgiving and Christmas each year.

Twelfth Year of Homeschooling (Ages 16, 15, 13)

Bible: Continued as in past years, reading together, praying, memorizing scripture.

History: This was the year for civics, which is required at some point during grades 7-12. I waited until this year so we could study it together using the Alpha Omega series of books on the topic. We also read from *A History of US* by Joy Hakim and watched several movies on related topics. We really had a great time learning about our Constitution, the branches of government, and current events. Our oldest son developed a strong interest in politics, which continues today.

From this point on in our homeschooling, each child worked more independently. Aside from history and Bible, all subjects were individualized.

Grade 11: Our oldest son, Aldan

English: Aldan worked through *Essay Intensive* (Institute for Excellence in Writing) to improve his writing skills and prepare for the SAT exam. *Writer's Inc.* by Great Source was another excellent resource.

Financial Accounting: Because Aldan told us he desired to continue in our business, we decided accounting would be a much better choice of math, rather than calculus. We found a college level course on computer CD called *Professor in a Box: Financial Accounting* by Dr. Michael Licata. The course proved to be both informative and challenging. He completed two-thirds of the material to receive his credit for math.

Chemistry/Meat Science: Now that we knew our son's future career goals, we could customize his final homeschool years to benefit him more specifically. We used *The Great Courses: Chemistry* from The Teaching Company as a half credit course in the basic principles of chemistry. My husband, who minored in meat science at the University of Tennessee, felt it would be beneficial to have a college textbook on meat processing. So, we located one on-line. Our son learned some background chemistry along with topics in meat processing. Both subjects together formed his science credit for the year.

Meat Processing Apprenticeship: Our son completed his school work Monday through Thursday and worked in our shop and on our farm Fridays and Saturdays. Over the course of the year, he learned sausage making, retail marketing, meat cutting, cheese making, and farming.

<u>Physical Education:</u> Varsity wrestling, wrestling camp

<u>4-H:</u> Aldan continued in 4-H Shotgun, Pig, and Beef clubs. He served as president of the Beef Club and his pig earned Champion at the local grange fair.

Other activities included: hunting (one of his passions), snowboarding, snowmobiling, a logging field trip, a class with a chef, and helping a friend who was battling cancer with his farm work.

Grades 9/10: Our middle child, Elizabeth

Elizabeth decided she wanted to complete two years of high school in one year's time. She had already earned two high school credits for math (she had completed both Algebra I and II prior to this year), so she wanted to double up on her sciences and English courses. She decided she felt led to become a practical nurse, so we planned her courses accordingly.

<u>English and Composition (Grade 9):</u> Elizabeth completed over 60 grammar lessons in the *Daily Grams* (Phillips) text and composed a twenty-six-page play. Additionally, she read numerous works of literature and the Bible.

<u>Literature and Composition (Grade 10):</u> For this second credit, Elizabeth enjoyed even more literature, composed a short story, an expository essay, and some narratives. She utilized the *Institute for Excellence in Writing*: *Essay Intensive* curriculum to fine tune her composition skills.

<u>Math:</u> She completed a geometry course using *Teaching Textbook*, opened her own checking account, obtained a debit card, and reconciled her bank account each month.

<u>Science:</u> Elizabeth earned two credits by completing over two-thirds of Apologia's Chemistry and Biology textbooks, including labs, study guides, and tests.

<u>Spanish:</u> Elizabeth earned a foreign language credit by working in the *Rosetta Stone* Spanish program for at least 120 days.

Other activities for Elizabeth included: three 4-H clubs (Vice President of the Pig Club, Treasurer of the Beef Club, member of Shotgun Club), field hockey at the public school, sewing, working in the shop and on the farm, caring for our cheeses, and maintaining her chickens.

At the grange fair she earned Reserve Champion Showman for both the Beef and Pig Clubs. Elizabeth attended the 4-H State Days Camp, hunted with her dad, worked Fridays and Saturdays in our store, and went skiing and snowmobiling.

Grade 7: Our youngest son, Luke

<u>English:</u> Included literature, composition, grammar, spelling, and handwriting. This was the first year of the big red *Easy Grammar* book, and we continued working on handwriting because it was much needed.

Materials utilized: *Institute for Excellence in Writing* by Andrew Pudewa, *Write Source 2000* by Pat Sebranek, *Easy Grammar Plus* (Phillips), *Apples Daily Spelling Drills for Secondary Students* by Susan Kemmerer, and a handwriting book to practice cursive writing.

<u>Math:</u> Luke had our usual 7th grade break from all *Saxon* math. He completed work on *Algebra ½* (*Saxon*), but also paid bills, wrote checks, and continued his cranberry relish business (figuring out costs and profits).

<u>Science:</u> He enjoyed another year full of hands-on activities, including experiments we found on the internet, Snap Circuits, and reloading shot-gun shells. He enjoyed several science books about the rain forest, small inventions, health topics, and simple machinery.

Other activities for Luke included: football, guitar lessons, caring for all the pigs on the farm, salting all the deer hides, working in the store,

4-H Pig and Shotgun Clubs, hunting (he harvested a deer with his bow and arrow), snowboarding, and snowmobiling.

This year our family enjoyed a trip to New Hampshire for some fun in the snow, then we went to Florida where we toured a logging operation and visited St. Augustine.

Thirteenth Year of Homeschooling (Ages 17, 16, 14)

This year of homeschooling proved to be the most difficult year for us as a family. At the beginning of the year, our children's dear sweet friend from 4-H passed away. She had been extremely close friends with both our daughter and our older son. The tragedy of her death shook our family more than we could have imagined. Looking back, I am amazed we accomplished anything academic this school year. The spiritual and emotional battles were extremely difficult. God is faithful! Little by little, year by year, healing came and joy seeped back into our lives.

We were especially thankful for our close emotional bonds formed over our years of living and learning together. I cannot imagine how much more difficult navigating this painful season would have been had we not had our children at home. This year, more than ever, made us really reflect on our priorities and the shortness of our time here on earth. We were reminded to keep the truly important things first in our lives.

Grade 12: Aldan

Aldan had signed up to take an introductory business class at the community college. After the trauma of losing his dear friend, we withdrew him from the class. College could wait. He needed time at home to heal, and he did not need any extra pressure placed upon him.

Aldan read excellent literature and completed several different genres of composition to fulfill this final English requirement, which was really his only needed credit for graduation. As an extra math credit, he completed a personal finances course using *Stewardship: Biblical*

Foundations by Math-U-See, managed his own checking account, and researched and purchased his own truck. Aldan spent even more time working with his father in the shop and on the farm this year, earning credits for small business management and meat processing.

He was voted as one of the captains of his varsity wrestling team, which finished the season as league champions. We will never forget the exciting night when Aldan pinned his opponent and sealed the team's victory in their biggest dual match of the season. On the late ride home from the team state championship, the chartered bus broke down. Aldan was able to use athletic tape to fix a leaking hose and get the bus safely to a spot where another bus could pick them up. The local newspaper wrote up a little story about our very own "wrestling handyman." Now that's a great homeschool success story!

Aldan won a special wrestling award for exceptional character, integrity, and hard work. The award came with a scholarship and was presented at the public school's senior recognition night. Although he never attended a single class at public school, Aldan sat on stage with other award-winning students. It was such a fun night!

We continued to read the Bible together this year. We read some of Virkler's *Dialogue with God* and learned about listening to hear God's voice and how to use journaling as a tool. Other than for Bible, Aldan was completely independent in his studies. I worked with the younger two children on history and together we read *Exploring World History* by Ray Notgrass.

Grade 11: Elizabeth

English: Elizabeth read books in various genres, studied grammar utilizing Ankar's *Grammar: Step by Step*, and looked into literary analysis with A Beka Book *World Literature* text. She continued to improve her vocabulary and spelling with A Beka Book's materials.

Math: Elizabeth completed our Ely graduation requirement of a course in Stewardship. She utilized the same texts as her brother: *Stewardship* (Math U See) and *Stewardship: Biblical Foundations* by Steve Demme.

We really liked these books for their excellent presentation of practical concepts as well as for the biblical component. The text covered personal finance (earning money, percent, taxes, banking, checking, interest, investing, budgeting, credit cards, comparison shopping), automotive (purchase, operation, mechanics, insurance), buying and maintaining a home, and other relevant topics. Elizabeth read each chapter and listened to a computer CD lesson, completed two workbook assignments, then took a final test on each chapter. In the biblical foundations book, she read a chapter and recorded a short summary in her notebook of the principles she learned for the day. All three of our children completed this same course. We felt it was so important for them to learn practical skills about handling their money in addition to recognizing the way God wanted them to think about and manage their finances. We are thankful to say that all three of our children have learned to handle their money well. They tithe, save, give, and spend in a biblical manner. This course was definitely time well spent!

Elizabeth put her training to excellent use as she researched, negotiated and purchased her first vehicle, a cute white Jeep. She also maintained and balanced her own checking account.

Science: In preparation for her future training as a nurse, Elizabeth studied anatomy and physiology using Apologia's text, *The Human Body: Fearfully and Wonderfully Made*. As one of her laboratory exercises, Elizabeth and her father dissected a market-sized hog. This was one of the clear benefits of farm life! She volunteered over 94 hours at the local hospital and shadowed a physical therapist for a day.

Spanish: Elizabeth completed her second credit as she continued with the *Rosetta Stone* computer program in Spanish.

Other activities: 4-H Pig Club (President), 4-H Beef Club (Secretary), 4-H Shotgun Club, working in the shop and on the farm, caring for chickens and cows, baking, cooking, and housekeeping.

Elizabeth really had enough credits to graduate this year, but we thought it would be best for her to have another year at home before moving on to nursing school or whatever the Lord had for her next. She was only sixteen years old, and we thought it would be beneficial for her to take a year to explore some areas of interest before moving forward.

Grade 8: Luke

English: Literature, vocabulary, spelling, poetry, *Jump In: A Workbook for Reluctant and Eager Writers* by Sharon Watson, *Easy Grammar Plus* (Phillips).

Math: *Key to Algebra*, books 1-3 (Rasmussen), *Pre-Algebra Concepts* (Fisher).

Science: *Matter & Motion in God's Universe* (A Beka Book), *TOPS Learning Systems: Floating and Sinking* by Ron Marson. This was an educational and fun activity-based book.

Luke cared for all of the pigs on our farm. He won Grand Champion Fitter for his neatly groomed pig at the fair, and he won a Mid-Atlantic Farm Credit award for excellence in animal science.

Art: *Looking at Pictures* by Joy Richardson, origami projects, *How to Draw and Paint Hoofed Animals* by Walter Wilwerding.

Other activities: 4-H Pig and Shotgun Clubs, football and wrestling (he broke his thumb in the first tournament and missed most of the season) at the local junior high school, landscaping for a neighbor, salting all of our deer hides, working in the shop and on the farm.

At the end of this school year, we celebrated our first graduation and made a big deal out of it. A pig roast, some tents and tables, yard games and volleyball, a beautiful cake, and plenty of friends and family made it a festive occasion. We displayed all our son's portfolios on a big table along with his awards and a laptop with a continuously looping slideshow of childhood memories and milestones. Guests were asked to write something meaningful for our son, and I compiled the cards and notes into a scrapbook for him to keep. For each of our children we had the same kind of big party. It gave us a special way to acknowledge all of their hard work and achievements over the years.

Fourteenth Year of Homeschooling (Ages 17, 15)

Our oldest started classes in small business management on a part-time schedule at the community college and worked full-time in our business.

Grade 12: Elizabeth

Elizabeth only had to complete credits in English and history to graduate. For English, she read literature and utilized an on-line writing tutor for guidance in literary analysis. She researched the differences between becoming a registered nurse (RN) and a practical nurse (LPN) and wrote a paper to share her discoveries. This process aided her in making her final decision to become an LPN. Additionally, Elizabeth learned about Clara Barton, a Civil War nurse, and composed a twelve-page research paper on her life, thus earning a history credit as well.

She volunteered at the hospital, cared for a friend's elderly mother-in-law, worked in our shop, and worked at a local breakfast restaurant. She continued with 4-H Pig Club (President) and Shotgun Club.

During the course of the year, Elizabeth researched the requirements for nursing school, studied for her entrance exam (which she passed with flying colors), applied and was accepted. She graduated officially in January, but we waited until May to celebrate her accomplishments with another big party.

Grade 9: Luke

Bible: We continued with our usual Bible reading.

English and History: *A Beautiful Feet* study guide of US History provided Luke with a literature-based history curriculum. *Daily Grams* (Phillips), *Vocabulary Cartoons* (New Monic Books Inc.), and materials from the Institute for Excellence in Writing aided Luke with his English studies.

Math: Saxon's *Algebra I*, Larry Burkett's *The World's Easiest Pocket Guide to Getting Your First Credit Card.*

Science: *Exploring Creation with Biology* (Apologia).

Luke completed experiments with two other homeschooled friends working on the same materials. At the end of the school year, we purchased a study guide for the CLEP exam. Luke passed, earning 6 college credits for Biology to save for a later date.

Spanish I: *Rosetta Stone* computer program.

Physical Education: JV wrestling team.

Other Activities: 4-H Pig and Shotgun Clubs, wrestling camp, hunting in South Dakota with Dad, salting deer hides, working in the shop, farm work, caring for cheeses, cranberry relish business, factory tours (BMW cars, gun factory), the Franklin Institute and the Dead Sea Scrolls, sporting clay shooting, tour of the Battleship NJ, EPCOT and Animal Kingdom (Florida), hunting, feeding the homeless in Philadelphia, 4-wheeler camping trips, and attending the grange fair.

Fifteenth Year of Homeschooling (Age 16)

Our oldest son continued to work in our business, taking classes part-time at the community college. Our middle child enrolled in a twelve-month LPN program at the community college. Since she had clinical experience two days per week and classroom courses the other three days, I had some special time home with our youngest.

Grade 10: Luke

Bible: Continued as in past years.

English: *Institute for Excellence in Writing* continued to help Luke write across the curriculum, *Vocabulary Cartoons* by New Monic Books increased his vocabulary, *Simply... Writing the Five-Paragraph Essay* (Pathways) taught Luke to write effective essays, *Step-by-Step Grammar Volume I: Basic Grammar* (Ankers) instructed him in grammar and the parts of speech and in diagramming sentences, *Research in Increments* (Kemmerer) provided guidance on research techniques and notetaking.

History: *A Literature Approach to US and World History* (Beautiful Feet) literature-based history curriculum.

Science: We started with a computer-based chemistry course. Midway into the course we found the computer program increasingly difficult to navigate through, so we switched to Apologia's *Exploring Creation with Chemistry* text.

Math: Teaching Textbook *Geometry*.

Spanish: *Rosetta Stone* computer course.

Physical Education: Varsity wrestling team; won the Die Hard Award for the hardest working team member.

Other Activities: 4-H Pig Club (President), Grange Fair, 4-H Shotgun Club, salted 1900 deer hides, worked in the butcher shop, cared for our pigs, continued cranberry relish business and lawn care for neighbor, completed roofing project with Dad and brother, hunting in PA and Kansas, snowmobiling in NH, skiing, earned driver's license, negotiated a deal and purchased first truck.

Sixteenth Year of Homeschooling (Age 17)

Our oldest son continued working full-time and studying part-time. Our daughter took a full-time position in a nursing home. After three months, she decided she liked nursing, but did not love it. She switched to part-time at the nursing home and part-time at our shop. After several years, she concluded that she really loved working in our business. She decided to maintain her nursing license but came to work for us full-time with her older brother.

Our youngest was still unsure of God's direction in his life; however, he felt the pull to go to college away from home. We all prayed about it and discerned the same path for him. With this in mind, we decided he should take some community college courses and learn how to navigate higher level classes with other teachers besides Mom.

Grade 11: Luke

Bible: In addition to reading the Bible together and praying, Luke and I read *The Battlefield of the Mind* by Joyce Meyer, which was extremely beneficial in helping us learn to take our thoughts captive as God desires. I was blessed to have one-on-one time with our youngest, especially since he had planned to leave home to attend college in the near future. Luke read *In Search of a Help Meet* by Michael Pearl, a Christian book about choosing a future wife carefully.

English: Luke took his first community college class in English and earned an A! He also read books at home to fulfill the literature requirement for his homeschool English credit.

Math: *Saxon Algebra II.*

Science: Luke completed a half credit course in physics with the Apologia text. His other half credit was a geology course by Alpha Omega.

Social Studies: A half credit was earned in American government (A Beka Book). Another half credit was earned in economics using *Whatever*

Happened to Penny Candy? by Richard Maybury and its accompanying study guide, *A Bluestocking Guide: Economics* by Jane Williams.

<u>Physical Education:</u> Varsity wrestling team. Luke placed in sectionals and districts and qualified for regionals, an impressive feat for someone only starting the sport in high school. He had broken both bones in his forearm the previous spring and had surgery where plates and screws were secured to his two bones. Luke battled back to regain his grip and the strength in his arm. Luke earned the team award for most improved wrestler.

<u>Other Activities:</u> Luke continued in the 4-H Pig (Vice President) and Shotgun Clubs, won Grand Champion Fitter at the Grange Fair, shot a 300-pound wild boar, and continued salting deer hides and working in the shop.

At the end of this school year and after visiting several colleges, Luke discerned one of the Christian schools we visited was most likely the place for him. He filled out his on-line application and was accepted.

Seventeenth and Final Year of Homeschooling (Age 18)

For the first half of his senior year, Luke took three community college courses: Effective Speaking, English Composition, and a course on computer operating systems. These courses were transferable to a four-year university. By taking three classes at once, Luke learned how to begin to succeed in a college setting and handle upper level academics. He was able to learn how to navigate the college's on-line platform for managing assignments and how to handle deadlines and final exams. His three courses went extremely well; Luke even made the Dean's list!

Luke and I continued reading the Bible together at home during the three days he did not have community college classes. We also read some of Virkler's *Dialogue with God*. I enjoyed the special one-on-one time together during this final year of homeschooling.

For the second semester, Luke finished up his homeschool English credit with some extra literature, vocabulary, and composition. Much of his writing included scholarship essays, and he earned several scholarship awards. He also completed the mandatory Ely stewardship course, worked in our shop, salted deer hides, participated in 4-H, and was captain of the varsity wrestling team where he finished his season placing fifth in the region. Luke was invited to the public school Senior Recognition Night, just like his older brother. He won the same character award and scholarship, plus an additional wrestling award. We finished out the school year with a family trip to Germany to an international convention for meat processors. When we returned, it was Luke's turn for his graduation celebration.

CHAPTER 6

Running the Race

Getting off to a Good Start

EACH STAGE, EACH day, each moment is passing, and nothing stays the same forever, except for Christ. If you are having a great school year, enjoy it but realize it will not always stay this way; a difficult one, take heart it will not be like this forever. As the Bible says, **"There is an appointed time for everything. And there is a time for every event under heaven" (Ecclesiastes 3:1).**

I remember when I first became a mom. For the first month or so, I can remember holding my infant son and looking into his beautiful eyes and thinking, *I am a mom. Wow, I am a mom!* After more than 26 years of only caring for myself, now I was responsible for this tiny helpless baby who had grown inside of me. Amazing! Becoming a parent is a big adjustment and a wonderful blessing. The Bible says, **"Behold, children are a gift of the Lord, the fruit of the womb is a reward" (Psalms 127:3).**

While children are an incredible blessing and gift, they are also a huge responsibility, and they require a tremendous amount of work, energy, time, and resources. When our children were small, I recall feeling as if I would never sleep through the night again. Surely, I was the only one in the world awake at 2 a.m.! Well-wishing, more seasoned parents would admonish us to relish the days of having young children, for they understood how quickly they would grow up. In the moment, it seemed that time went ever so slowly, but days became months and too soon, months became years.

Now, I too, am a seasoned parent with grown children, and I understand exactly what these well-meaning people attempted to convey. Time marches on. I DID try to enjoy all of the days and the moments while we raised our children. I often reminded myself to treasure the time we had together. Looking back, it still passed much too quickly. Life is short, and we all need to make the most of the days the Lord has given us.

So, what advice would I give to parents with young children, not yet of school age? First, I would advise you to constantly seek our Heavenly Father. Only in abiding in Him will you be the parents He has called you to be. Ask Him for wisdom. He promises to give it to you (**James 1:5,6**). The more time you spend with your Heavenly Father, the more you will become like Him. He is the perfect parent. He will show you what to teach your children, how to train them, and how to correct them. Read His Word, pray for yourselves as parents, and pray for your children.

Secondly, I would tell young parents to set limits for your children. Teach your children to obey you cheerfully and immediately, and they will then learn to obey God as they grow older. As the Bible instructs: **"Children, obey your parents in the Lord, for this is right" (Ephesians 6:1).**

Love your children and seek always to guide their hearts, not merely their external behavior. I love the books, *Shepherding a Child's Heart* by Tedd Tripp and *Hints on Child Training* by Henry Clay Trumball because they both give practical insight and wisdom in molding a child's heart.

Finally, trust God and give yourself grace. God is faithful, perfect, and loving. He covers our weaknesses and fills in the gaps. No human being can be a perfect parent. If you truly learn to do your best and trust God with the results, you will be better able to enjoy your children and the whole process of training them.

When our children were young, we played with them and enjoyed them. We took them with us grocery shopping or on errands. We visited grandparents and invited other families to meals in our home. We read out loud to our children, and we included them in household projects.

As they were able, we gave them little jobs to do to "help" us. When my kids were around the ages of six, eight, and ten, I recall thinking how helpful they were and how much fun it was to spend time with them. They were clever, funny, diligent, and a pleasure to be around. I was so thankful we had taken the time to train our children.

No Perfect Parents

When your children are under the age of five, much of your parenting involves caring for their physical needs. During this time, you are also teaching them: how to love, how to talk, how to walk, how to care for their bodies, how to eat and drink, how to share, how to obey, how to listen, and how to interact with people. Whether you realize it or not, you ARE their teacher from the very beginning. When they reach the age of five, you have a decision to make; will you keep them home and continue to train them up, or will you delegate the teaching to someone else for the majority of the day?

Ask God for wisdom and direction, then trust Him to guide you. Talk to your spouse, make your decision together, then step out in faith, not fear.

There are no perfect parents. You will make mistakes. There will be gaps in your children's education no matter which option you choose. All of this is okay! God will guide you; He will help you; He will forgive you and pick you up when you fall short and will love you and your children from now through eternity. We can ask God to fill in the gaps and trust Him to do it.

No one will love your children or invest as much in their upbringing as you will! Homeschooling gives you the opportunity to love and invest in your children in a way that pleases God.

Keep in Mind Long Term Goals

It's important to think through and pray about the long term goals you have for your children. For a time, they have been entrusted into your care. When they leave home someday, what do you hope and pray for them?

Writing your goals down is helpful. You can arrange them by categories: spiritual, character, physical, life skills, etc. When you are choosing new materials, making plans for the year, or hitting rough patches, you can always come back to your goals to remind yourself of the big picture as you guide your children through life.

A brief list of goals for your children upon leaving home could include:

- Salvation- a personal and growing relationship with God
- God's Word-reading, memorizing, studying, discussing
- Love God and hear His voice
- Character-obedience, repentance, generosity, honesty, integrity, diligence, service
- Work Ethic
- Relational Skills-with God, self, family, friends, and others
- Life Skills-chores, cooking, cleaning, home and car repair, use of tools, managing money
- Academic Skills- how to learn, reading, writing, math, etc.

Each year, you can write shorter term goals for each child. These short-term goals should always line up with your long-term goals; they are the little steps all along the way. At the end of the year, it can be encouraging to look back at the goals and see the growth each of your children has made, and it can be helpful in noticing which areas still need more work.

Know the Law

Every state has its own homeschool laws, and it is important to find out what your state requires of you. A great resource we used is the Home School Legal Defense Association (HSLDA), which is a legal organization with the purpose of protecting the parents' right to homeschool. They provide some free services, while other services are available to members only. The yearly family membership is reasonable, and during our homeschool years, we paid the yearly fee and looked at it as a donation to a worthy cause and an inexpensive insurance policy. HSLDA can provide you with the information regarding the homeschool laws you must follow in your own state. Of course, you can always look the laws up directly yourself or contact other homeschool organizations in your state to help you discern the requirements.

In preparing yourself for this journey, some of the questions you should answer are:

- **What is the mandatory school attendance age?** For instance, in Pennsylvania it is ages 8-17 (or until graduation, whichever comes first). If your child has never been enrolled in public school, you do not need to follow reporting requirements until he is 8 years old. If you live in the city of Philadelphia, if you are teaching a child who has been identified under the federal Individuals with Disabilities Education Act as needing special education services, or if you are withdrawing your child from public school, you should check the HSLDA website for your specific requirements.

- **Do you need to turn in any special papers?** Usually, you can contact your school administration office, and they can provide you with a packet of required documents to complete. Sometimes they may ask you for paperwork which is not mandated by law; this is where it is helpful to know the law and to have an HSLDA contact to answer any questions you may have. In short, prior to August 1, we were required to turn in a ***notarized affidavit***, our ***academic objectives*** for each of the required subjects, and ***medical and dental records. 180 days*** of school (or 900 logged hours for elementary/ 990 logged hours for secondary) were also mandatory. We always found it easier to keep track of days by using a calendar to highlight the days we completed any academic work or activities. We also utilized planners to document the work we completed in each subject area. At the end of the school year, we were required to ***meet*** *with a Pennsylvania certified teacher or evaluator* who would *interview* our child, check our *daily log* and *portfolio* of work, and write a letter to the school district certifying our child was receiving an appropriate education. In grades 3, 5, and 8, our children were required to take *standardized tests* and show the scores to our evaluator. Finally, prior to June 30, we needed to *submit a copy of our evaluator's letter* for each child to the school district.

Pennsylvania is one of the most restrictive homeschool states, so most likely you will not need to supply this much information if you homeschool in another state. At first the requirements may seem overwhelming, but they are not overly difficult to meet once you become familiar with them.

- **Is my child able to participate in extracurricular activities?** Pennsylvania law requires public schools to allow homeschool students living within the school district access to participation in any extracurricular activities including sports, clubs, drama, or music. Although our children greatly enjoyed playing sports on public school teams, some families prefer not to utilize any public school resources. It is a blessing to have the choice; however, some states do not require public schools to accommodate homeschoolers in this or in any other way.

Make a Plan

Once you have researched and complied with the state laws, you can select books and materials and make a plan for the year. We prayed, researched and selected materials, wrote our objectives, then planned week to week, always adjusting if needed. For example, if we knew we wanted to study early American history, we selected the books and materials we planned to use to help accomplish our objectives, but we did not write out a year's worth of lesson plans all at once. If we found new materials to add during the year or decided we did not like the original books we chose, then we had the freedom to change our plan. There are many wonderful homeschool teacher resources available which help make planning easier, especially for the beginning homeschool parent. Check out the chapter on our favorite materials and resources to help get you started with your research.

On-line public school has become a widely-used alternative to traditional homeschooling. If you enroll your children, the program usually supplies a computer and all books or support materials needed. Additionally, your children fall under the jurisdiction of the public school system and are subject to its requirements. If you decide to research this option, look carefully at the curriculum and be sure it is not undermining the very values you are working to instill in your children. Also, be certain that you want to adhere to the schedule and calendar of the program. Some parents like the "safety net" of the public school system and the ease of planning this approach affords; however, they may not realize that they are sacrificing their control over what, when, and how their children learn.

Keep it Simple

In choosing materials and making your plans, be sure to keep things simple so you will not feel too overwhelmed. If you like the books you are reading with your children and feel good about your plan, homeschooling will be easier and more pleasant for everyone. When kids are little, keep school time short. Include plenty of physical activities and incorporate chores into your day. Engaging in physical activity first usually helps children concentrate better.

Make learning as pleasant and fun as you can, and try to be flexible. Rarely did one of our homeschool days go as planned! Read the Bible daily and be sure you focus on character training issues as they come up. You may not finish all you had planned, but you will reap great rewards when you take the time to truly train up your children in God's ways. Do crafts, projects, library trips, chores, and life together. Don't forget to plan field trips into your schedule; if you plan them, they are more likely to occur.

Make a Schedule

Some people are more relaxed than others in their homeschooling approach. Whether you are a Type A personality and love organization or you have a more laid-back personality and you prefer a freer flowing approach, making a basic schedule can help keep you on track in meeting your goals. Below are some sample schedules to show you what a structured day might look like.

Sample schedule for children under the age of 8:
- Wake up, personal Bible and prayer time
- Brush teeth, dress, make bed
- Breakfast (we found including protein greatly helps concentration)
- Clean up, complete morning chores
- Bible time-read, discuss, narrate back, recite memory verses, sing, pray
- Phonics- one-on-one while other children play or color
- Writing-copying, handwriting, journals, thank you notes
- Snack or break
- Math-use plenty of manipulatives and activities
- Read aloud
- Chores
- Lunch (school work is complete by this time)
- Play time- children can have quiet reading or room time if little ones (or Mom!) need a nap
- Errands, outside activities, take a walk
- Dinner prep for Mom and play time for kids
- Dinner and clean up
- Family time
- Bedtime

Sample schedule for children beyond the age of 8:
- Personal Bible time
- Breakfast
- Chores

- Bible time
- History-read aloud, color, map work, projects, writing, ...
- Math and language-kids work individually, parent helps one-on-one
- Science-read aloud, projects, experiments, nature walks
  (You can work on science and history on alternate days, 2 days each with Fridays off)
- Art, music, physical education, or projects
- Lunch
- Chores
- Play, finish remaining work, free time
- Dinner
- Family time
- Bedtime

➤ Complete Bible, history, science together
➤ Individualize language and math instruction
➤ Link writing to Bible, history, and science studies when possible

Remember:

- Love your children; spend time with them.
- Set limits for your children.
- Pray, seek God's wisdom, and discuss with your spouse.
- Remember that no parent is perfect; give yourself grace.
- Set goals.
- Know the law.
- Make a plan; keep it simple.
- Set a schedule, but be flexible.
- With God's help, you can do it!

Staying the Course

I recall one homeschool convention speaker share that we have the years from the time of their birth through age 12 to hold our children close.

Beyond age 12, there is usually a clear relationship adjustment. At the time, I remember thinking I disagreed because my own children felt so close to my heart, and although the oldest was maybe 13, it felt as if our relationship would always be this way. Now that all of my children are much past 12, I have experienced the reality of that speaker's words in my own life and have observed it in the lives of others as well.

When our children are young and we have a large amount of control over what they can and cannot do, it is difficult to envision the days ahead when they will pull away to become independent. The truth is that this is a gradual process which begins at birth. As our children grow, they move toward independence; this is God's design for them. As parents, we need to guide our children and hold them with open hands up to our Heavenly Father. Gradually, we need to release them so they can be the individuals God created them to be. Children naturally pull away from their parents in their teen years. They need to step out and learn who they are as individuals, and separating in some degree from parents is a necessary part of this process.

While the letting go can be difficult for parents, it is necessary and good. If we can launch our children into this world as capable adults who have a living and active relationship with Jesus Christ as Lord and Savior, and if they are supporting themselves, are contributing to society, and are fulfilling their callings, then we will have indeed played a part in leaving a wonderful legacy.

So, in this "sweet spot" of the middle years of homeschooling, enjoy your children. These are exciting and fun family years. Now is the time to laugh and play together, to live life together as you create memories and build heart connections. Now is the time to speak into the lives of your children, to share those things you deem truly important. Now is the time to study the topics and read the books you feel are paramount. Now is the time to keep communication open and flowing.

Now is also the time to increase your prayers for your children. Had I known then what I do now, I would have stepped up my prayer life for my kids from the time they were small. It seemed as if everything was going so smoothly and was so much fun that I was lulled into a sense we had somehow arrived at a point where we could coast. When our children entered their teen years and we were confronted with the tragic loss of their dear friend, I realized that praying for my children needed to be a more fervent and consistent part of my role.

So, pray, pray, pray! Pray for yourselves as parents to have wisdom. Pray for all aspects of the lives of your children. Pray they will have good and godly friends, wise and loving mentors, discernment, purity, and direction. Stormie Omartian's book, *The Power of a Praying Parent*, is a wonderful resource. I love praying a prayer from her book each day because it reminds me to address all areas of my children's lives. God can move mountains for your children, and your prayers can make an incredible difference.

Enjoy these years, for they are truly special. They will not last forever, but don't be discouraged. If you make those heart connections and keep communication open, your children will want to share important parts of their lives with you. One day, you may find as we have found, your adult children have become your dearest friends.

Finishing Well: The High School Years

By the time your children reach their high school years, you will have a good idea of their strengths and weaknesses, their likes and dislikes, and their learning styles. At this point, some children may have a passion and a dream for what they hope to do in the future, while other children have no idea. These final years of homeschooling are full of exciting changes and opportunities. Now is the time to take advantage of the ability to customize each child's education; homeschooling does not need to be a one-size-fits-all method.

If your children know what they hope to do in the future, you can prayerfully help them plan. Their high school courses can be geared toward their goals. Our oldest son wanted to continue in our business, so he studied accounting and meat science and did an apprenticeship with Dad. Will college be part of their plans? If so, they can start at a community college or take college courses on-line while still in high school. You can start with one course, and then gradually add on others. By the time they are ready to leave, your children will be well prepared for college level work and have extra credits to transfer into the school of their choice (with some limitation, depending upon the school selected). Some students complete their associate's degree while still in high school. One friend we know completed her bachelor's degree by high school graduation! She utilized an on-line program that helped guide her through the necessary courses and exams to obtain her degree.

If your children are unsure of what is next, help them explore to see potential areas of interest. When our daughter thought she might like to be a nurse, she volunteered at a hospital, interviewed people in the medical field, and took a job caring for an elderly friend. Your children can try different jobs or apprenticeships, shadow professionals in a field of their interest, and take courses at a community college or on-line. You can prayerfully guide your children to help them discern the next steps God is calling them to take.

"The mind of man plans his way, but the Lord directs his steps" (Proverbs 16:9).

Beyond Homeschooling

Although our homeschool years have passed, the lessons continue. God constantly reminds me of ways we trained our children in the past as an example of how He is training us presently. Just as we prepared our children for adulthood, He is getting us ready for eternity. We loved making our kids happy along the way by giving them "good gifts." But, we kept their ultimate good in mind. A child whining about completing chores could have been made instantly happier if we had removed the requirement. But, we knew our children needed to learn how to work hard and how to choose to do it joyfully. Making the path too easy, free of trials and struggle, would not have prepared them for a happy adult life. Skipping math or reading would have left them limited in their later choices for college or vocation. So, we stuck to our guns, whining and all, and helped them learn responsibility, diligence, and integrity.

As I sat in church singing the lyrics to a new popular worship song, it hit me: *I'm no longer a slave to fear; I am a child of God. I'm no longer a slave to fear; I am a child of God....* God strongly impressed this fact upon me; I AM HIS CHILD. Wow! I realized I wanted to search the Bible to find the references to God as my Father and me as His child. In those moments, God revealed to me that all the years of loving and training my children were part of my classroom time in learning how much my Heavenly Father loves me and how many blessings, privileges, joys, challenges, and surprises are mine simply because I enjoy my status as a child of the King.

As parents, we pour our hearts and souls into our children. They receive our time, energy, love, and resources. Day by day and year by year, they captivate our hearts. Nothing brings us greater pleasure than to share fellowship and joy with our children. Nothing breaks our hearts more than when our relationship with them is strained, or they pull away from us.

God loves to give us good gifts. He longs to make us happy and to bless us. But, He sees eternity stretching before us, and He is preparing us for it. Sometimes this means withholding a gift or delaying a promise until His perfect timing.

We have celebrated victories with our children when dreams have been fulfilled or goals have been met. Those have been sweet and rewarding moments. We have also walked with our children through times of great sorrow and disappointment. In those times, our hearts have ached with them.

As we think back on raising our children, we remember how we desired to give them "good gifts" when it was appropriate and beneficial. We disciplined them and trained them for their ultimate good. They have grown into godly, capable individuals, prepared for God's best in their lives. So, along with our children, in the good times and in the difficult times, we have chosen to trust. God is always good. He is always loving and kind. He knows what is best for His kids.

God is always teaching us, training us up in the way we should go, preparing us for what lies ahead. He is a good Father, and along the way, He gives us good gifts and sprinkles our path with encouragement and joy just when we need it.

And so, these child-rearing, homeschooling years have done more than prepare our children to be God-loving, God-following, capable adults; they have taught us more about how God sees us. We now have a fleshed-out example. And to think, our love for our children is only a fraction of His love for us!

While the homeschooling chapter of our lives has ended, parenting never does. Our relationships with our children change and mature, but they are eternal. Our homeschooling is complete, but God still has lessons to teach us. Many times, I reflect on the training of our children as I try to discern God's present lesson for me.

Homeschooling has not always been easy. It has required sacrifices and dying to self. But, not for one minute do we regret our decision to homeschool! We thank God for keeping us on this course.

Homeschooling will stretch you. It will bring you frustration and joy. Most of all, homeschooling will give you the gift of TIME with your children. Time to love them, time to know them, time to train them up in God's ways. You will all learn, fail, succeed, laugh, cry, and grow together. You will have time to build a strong foundation in the Lord, time to read and live out God's Word, time to forge strong relationships, and time to equip your children to launch out into their future. The blessings will stretch on throughout your lifetime and beyond!

CHAPTER 7

Favorite Books and Materials

Resources that have Impacted My Life

O VER THE YEARS, the Lord has used various books and materials to greatly impact my walk with Him and the ways in which I navigate this life. The Bible, of course, is the greatest book of all eternity. It contains everything we need to know, everything needed to walk in fullness of life. I have heard of stories of people who have read the Bible and only the Bible, nothing else. Others have chosen to read only as much of other books as they do of the Bible. I respect these choices and can see the wisdom in them. I have found that certain books have allowed me to see biblical truths in a way I had somehow missed from the Word directly. Books have been mentors to me, and I am thankful for those who have labored to write them so that others might be blessed by wisdom they have gained. Judging from the number of Christian books sold each year, I feel certain I am in good company. The following is a partial list of some of my favorite resources:

The Bible
Without a doubt, the greatest book ever written. God's Word is alive and powerful and able to change lives! The one book to choose if you could choose only one.

My Utmost for His Highest by Oswald Chambers
This is a daily devotional, originally published in 1927. I prefer the original rich language, although more modern translations are available.

This book has a Bible verse and devotional for each day of the year. After years of reading it, each passage still seems new and challenging to my walk with the Lord. My first copy was given to me by one of my fourth-grade students, and is now a little worn and tattered as it sits on a deep window sill in our home. I cannot tell you how many days the words from that book have been exactly what I needed to hear. The pages are full of wisdom and of love for our Creator. Powerful!

Created to Be His Help Meet by Debi Pearl
This book was written by a wife, for wives-an older woman teaching younger women just as the Word directs in **Titus 2:3-5**. Debi writes in a straightforward, no-nonsense manner, and she bases her teaching on God's directions to women in the Bible. I have found this work affirming in some areas, convicting in others. Mostly, it has given me a solid picture of God's design for wives.

Turning Hearts, and *I Saw the Angel in the Marble*
by Chris and Ellyn Davis
These CD's and book talk about seeing our children as God sees them, drawing out their gifts and talents, and guiding them into their own unique futures. The words in these CD's set me free from the constraints of a one-size-fits-all education. I was finally able to embrace our own unique family lifestyle, and I was freer to let my children develop at their own pace. Nothing transformed our homeschooling as much as the truths in these materials did.

Battlefield of the Mind by Joyce Meyer
This book offers powerful and life changing concepts! It expresses how I must choose to take my thoughts and words captive to God's truths. By God's strength, I can decide what I will think on and what will come forth from my mouth. Changes in these areas can be totally life transforming.

Dialogue with God by Mark Virkler
This book offers a wonderful aid in learning to discern the voice of God in your life. It challenged me to take journaling to a new level, whereby I could better understand what God wants to teach me.

The Power of a Praying Wife and *The Power of a Praying Parent* by Stormie Omartian
Each book contains chapters on a different aspect of our husband or our children's lives that we can pray about. Each chapter ends with a prayer laced with scripture about the topic at hand. I read these aloud to God almost every day. When I get to the last prayer in the book, I restart at the beginning. We can never have too much prayer!

Crossingumc.org Sermons by Dr. Scott McDermott
Our family has been blessed to call Dr. Scott McDermott both pastor and friend. He currently serves as lead pastor of the Washington Crossing United Methodist Church. He is a godly man, committed to prayer and the study and teaching of God's Word. Pastor Scott has an incredible gift of teaching, and he presents biblical truths in creative, practical, and engaging ways. His Holy Spirit-inspired teachings have helped our entire family grow spiritually by leaps and bounds.

The following list of Christian biographies inspired and challenged me to see how stepping out of the "comfort zone" leads believers into their destinies in Christ:

Kisses from Katie: A Story of Relentless Love and Redemption by Katie Davis Majors
A 19-year-old girl leaves her comfortable life here in the U.S. to love the people of Uganda. In her book, Katie shares portions of her journal revealing her joys and struggles as she steps into her calling. This is an inspiring and powerful story.

The Hiding Place by Corrie Ten Boom
A watchmaker's daughter hides Jews in her home in Austria during WWII. She and her family risk their lives to do what they know is right. Be prepared for a heart-pounding, emotional, and riveting story!

God's Smuggler by Brother Andrew
The story of a rebellious boy, seeking adventure, who is captured by God for the greatest adventures of his life: smuggling Bibles into closed countries and witnessing God's continual and miraculous provisions.

Greater Works and other books by Smith Wigglesworth
Wigglesworth was an illiterate plumber, born in 1859, who made himself available to Christ and was used by Him to work miracles and lead many to salvation. These are amazing stories of powerful faith.

Helpful Homeschool Organizations

- **CHAP: Christian Homeschool Association of PA (chaponline.com)**
  You can find information on the annual convention, sample forms for affidavits, audio recordings about various homeschool topics from past conventions, and other useful information and links.

- **HSLDA: Home School Legal Defense Association (hslda.org)**
  This national organization fights to keep homeschooling legal and available across our country and around the world. For an annual membership fee, you gain access to legal advice and help, should you need it, regarding homeschooling. You also have access to their numerous on-line resources. This group is definitely worth joining!

Catalogs and Websites for Homeschool Materials

- **Rainbow Resource Center (rainbowresource.com)**
  This is the phone book of all homeschool catalogs. Every year it gets thicker. It contains a massive number of homeschool materials,

including helpful descriptions for each item. If you order over a certain dollar amount, shipping is usually free. A caution here to the new homeschooler; the catalog can be a bit overwhelming.

- **CBD (Christianbook.com)**
  Many are already familiar with this Christian book website. They carry an extensive selection of homeschool materials and publish smaller homeschool catalogs with helpful descriptions and material reviews.

- **Beautiful Feet Books (bfbooks.com)**
  We loved these simple-to-use study guides which incorporate excellent works of literature. Check the website for topics and appropriate grade levels.

- **Sonlight (sonlight.com)**
  This company also uses literature-based instruction. I love their book suggestions according to topic.

Diploma Programs in Pennsylvania

- **Mason-Dixon Homeschoolers (mdhsa-pa.org)**
  I loved the flexibility of this program. The staff is helpful and caring, and the diploma and transcripts are professional looking. Also, the fees are extremely reasonable.

- **PA Homeschoolers (pahomeschoolers.com)**
  This group offers a diploma program as well as on-line classes and other helpful resources. The website provides numerous homeschool links.

- **Erie County Home Schoolers Diploma Association (echsdiploma.org)**
  This homeschool group offers yet another option for homeschoolers in Pennsylvania to earn a high school diploma.

Check with the Pennsylvania Department of Education for other accredited diploma programs. Each state is different, so you will need to know your state's homeschool laws and check its website or check in with HSLDA for more information.

Our Favorite Homeschool Resources

Following are some of the materials, arranged by topic, we found most useful and enjoyable.

Homeschool Helps/Christian Life and Character

Educating the Wholehearted Child by Clay and Sally Clarkson
This is a comprehensive book on home education, including approaches to homeschooling, learning styles, suggested materials and activities, and more. This is an excellent resource for anyone considering homeschooling!

For Instruction in Righteousness by Pam Forster
This is a wonderful resource for child training. This book is packed with scripture and is divided into categories to help you easily find what you need to encourage good behavior and attitudes and correct poor ones. I love how this book encourages parents to really look at the hearts of their children as they seek to correct and guide them in God's ways.

The Five Love Languages of Children: The Secret to Loving Children Effectively by Gary Chapman
For our children to feel truly loved, we must demonstrate their love languages. This is an important book for all relationships. It helped me learn how to best express love to each of my children in ways they could feel it.

Books on Christian Character to Read with your Children

Kingdom Parables by Christopher Lane
This text offers some of Jesus' parables, retold as stories with animals as the main characters. A fun way to get the concepts across.

Days on the Farm with Annette and Samuel by Teresa Morgan
This book provides sweet, short chapters containing stories about a Mennonite family and the life lessons encountered on their farm.

Missionary Stories with the Millers by Mildred A. Martin
This text contains short, inspiring biographies of missionaries written in a child-friendly manner. Each chapter starts with a world map highlighting the country in which the story is set.

Hero Tales by Dave and Neta Jackson
Each chapter of this book is a short biography of a different Christian hero.

In Search of a Help Meet by Michael Pearl
This book is written for an audience of young adult men. It details important points to consider in choosing a wife.

Phonics Instruction and Early Reading

Phonics Pathways by Dolores Hiskes
This text is simple and easy to use. It encompasses everything you need to teach reading, all in one book.

Teach Your Child to Read in 100 Easy Lessons by Siegfried Engelmann
This is a scripted manual for teaching beginning reading.

Explode the Code by Nancy Hall
This is a series of simple phonics workbooks where the child reads, writes, or marks an "x" for various exercises. We found these helpful for

young students who find the physical act of writing difficult because there is very little actual writing.

Bob Books by Bobby Lynn Maslen
These are simple and sequential books for beginning readers.

Doodle Loops by Sandy Baker
This book provides a fun way to practice beginning reading. The student reads a description containing five simple sentences, then draws a picture to illustrate.

Reading, Writing, Spelling, Grammar, Vocabulary

Five in A Row by Becky Jane Lambert
This is a helpful teacher's guide containing science, history, and language activities based on literature. Each lesson is focused on a different book. It is best for the elementary ages.

Beautiful Feet study guides by Rea Berg
These literature-based history guides are available in all age levels and for many historical topics. We loved these!

A Reason for Handwriting by Carol Ann Retzer and Eva Hoshino
These are Bible-based handwriting workbooks.

The WIN Program: Writing in Narrative by Dr. Leslie Simonson
These are simple writing workbooks which guide beginning writers in an easy step-by-step, non-threatening manner.

Language Lessons for the Elementary Child by Sandi Queen
This book offers daily language lessons that include picture study, copy work, narration, dictation, grammar, poetry, writing, and more. It is simple and easy to use.

Just Write by Elsie S. Wilmerding and Alexandra S. Bigelow
This workbook provides a step-by-step writing guide for the beginning writer. Students progress from writing sentences and paragraphs to stories.

Jump In: A Workbook for Reluctant and Eager Writers by Sharon Watson
For the middle school years, this student-friendly writing guide covers all aspects of the writing process and many different types of writing styles.

Institute for Excellence in Writing: Student Writing Intensive
by Andrew Pudewa
This series provides clear, step-by-step instruction in both writing structure and style. This program is intended to be used in conjunction with your other subject area studies. Many materials are available, but this is a great one to start with.

Simply… Writing the Five-Paragraph Essay by Pathways
This straightforward book walks the intermediate writer through the steps of a short essay. This is a great introduction to formal essay writing and can be used across the curriculum.

WriteGuide.com
(WriteGuide.com is now closed. It appears that Luxwritingcenter. com continues to provide writing instruction in a similar manner to WriteGuide.com.)
This excellent on-line writing tutorial is useful for any learning level. For a reasonable monthly fee, the student is assigned an individual writing tutor. You can even share the time between different students. You can ask the tutor to design a plan, or you can ask him to help you with a specific task or set of skills. On one occasion, we had the tutor walk our son through the process of a ten-page research paper, while he helped our daughter work on a composition. I love the fact that you can customize the lessons and the time period. Both student and parent can send one email per day, and the teacher emails once daily. The quality of the teaching was excellent; emails came with encouragement, explanations, examples, and instruction. This program was well worth the money!

Spelling Power by Beverly Adams-Gordon
This is one spelling book which can be used for all learning levels. Students take pretests to determine which words they need to learn. They form a spelling list from these selected words, then move through a series of activities to learn their correct spelling. I like this approach of studying only those words that needed to be learned, rather than performing activities on words that were already known. The parent needs to be available to give pre-tests and post-tests orally.

Calvert Spelling CD's by The Calvert School
These CD's offered a similar approach to *Spelling Power*, but everything is completed on the computer with no need for a parent to give tests. Some of the practice games are especially fun for the children.

Apples Daily Spelling Drills for Secondary Students by Susan Kemmerer
This is a great workbook for older students who struggle with spelling. It is written with this age group in mind, so it is not perceived as too childish.

Easy Grammar Plus by Wanda Phillips
This is a comprehensive grammar workbook. The student starts by learning all of the prepositions and completes one page per day. The text is both incremental and thorough. Our children completed these books over the course of seventh and eighth grades.

Daily Grams by Wanda Phillips
This was a nice, short daily grammar refresher workbook. Our children worked on a page per day: a grammar "vitamin."

Step-by-Step Grammar Volume I: Basic Grammar by Angela M. Ankers
We found these texts later in our homeschooling years. Just as the title suggests, these books are incremental. They offer a simple, non-threatening approach to grammar, which focuses on diagramming sentences based on parts of speech.

Editor in Chief workbooks by Critical Thinking Company
These are workbooks with short, interesting paragraphs for the student to practice editing skills.

A Word a Week Vocabulary Program by Teacher Created Resources
These books provide an interesting story for each vocabulary word. We enjoyed reading these aloud together, and the stories were memorable enough to make most words "stick."

Vocabulary Cartoons by New Monic Books
We found these books late in our homeschooling years but loved them. Our youngest son found them humorous. I am not sure if this book was the reason for his excellent vocabulary, but I am sure it helped!

Some Favorite Historical Fiction Read-Aloud Texts

Johnny Tremain by Esther Hoskins Forbes
This book is set in Boston during the outbreak of the American Revolution.

Toliver's Secret by Esther Wood Brady
Set during the American Revolution, this text shares the tale of a young girl who embarks on a mission to smuggle a message to George Washington.

The Bronze Bow by Elizabeth George Speare
This is the story of a young boy in Galilee during the time of Jesus.

The Witch of Blackbird Pond by Elizabeth George Speare
This story takes place in a Puritan colony in New England during the colonial period.

The Golden Goblet by Eloise Jarvis-McGraw
This book offers an exciting tale set in Ancient Egypt.

History Resources

Beautiful Feet Study Guides by Rea Berg
These guides can be used for literature, history, science, and geography topics.

The Story of the Middle Ages by Michael McHugh and John Southworth
This slim textbook contains very interesting and informative chapters on the Middle Ages.

Lifepac Civics by Alpha Omega Publishers
This series of booklets provides an excellent overview of Civics, including many original documents.

American Government in Christian Perspective by A Beka Book
This text provides a clear and interesting description of how the US government is organized and how the different branches function.

D'Aulaire's Book of Greek Myths by Edgar Parin D'Aulaire
This book is a compilation of interesting tales of Greek Myths. We were glad to expose our children to a small dose of these since many myths are referenced in our society.

Shakespeare Stories by Leon Garfield
This is a great resource for students who want to know the stories of Shakespeare but wish to read them in modern-day English. I know some of you may find it appalling to read anything other than the originals; however, this is a great tool for those seeking it.

Geography Songs produced by Audio Memory, written by Larry and Kathy Troxel
Audio Memory makes CD's with songs to learn many different topics. The tunes are catchy and really help students learn states, capitals, countries, continents, etc. in a fun and easy way. Plus, they provide a little extra music for those of us who struggle in this area.

A History of US by Joy Hakim
We found this to be a very interesting and engaging series of books on American history, complete with photographs, maps, and illustrations.

The Story of the World: History for the Classical Child: Volume 4: The Modern Age, and the accompanying activity book, by Susan Wise Bauer
I especially liked the outlines and maps provided in the activity book, as they were incredibly user-friendly.

Abraham Lincoln's World by Genevieve Foster
This interesting book paints a picture of what was happening around the world during the time Abraham Lincoln lived.

George Washington's World by Genevieve Foster
This book depicts life during the time George Washington lived.

Whatever Happened to Penny Candy? by Richard Maybury
This book offers a unique introduction to economics. We used this along with the study guide below.

A Bluestocking Guide to Economics by Jane A. Williams
This text serves as a wonderful companion to *Whatever Happened to Penny Candy?*

Math

Saxon by Saxon Publishers, written by John Saxon
These math textbooks and instructional CD-ROM are available in all levels. As new concepts are introduced, multiple practice problems are provided for the new concept, plus many problems which review concepts from past lessons. This incremental yet cumulative approach provides a very thorough education in mathematics. The CD-ROM provides instruction and serves as the teacher. Solution and test manuals are also available. We found this program to be clear, informative, and straightforward.

Teaching Textbook by Greg Sabouri

This program is similar to that of *Saxon*. The books are printed in a friendlier looking font and are extremely thick. We used this for Geometry because, at the time, *Saxon* included Geometry as part of Algebra I and Algebra II and we desired a complete course which included writing proofs. These are pricier than *Saxon* but are available on every level.

Key to... books by Steven Rasmussen

These are short, incremental workbooks arranged by topic (percent, fractions, decimals, etc.). We used these as reinforcement and review of key concepts.

Grocery Cart Math by Common Sense Press

These books are best suited for upper elementary level students. They provide practical, fun, educational math activities to complete while grocery shopping. We enjoyed using these occasionally as a supplement to our other math activities. Also, it was a nice distraction for our children, who did not particularly love coming along to the grocery store.

Stewardship: Biblical Foundations by Steven Demme

We required the completion of this practical, Bible-based math course for each of our children prior to graduation from high school. Our children really enjoyed this book and found it to be both practical and interesting. We especially liked the biblical component.

The World's Easiest Pocket Guide to Getting Your First Credit Card by Larry Burkett

This tiny book offered great information on credit cards. The author presents the benefits and drawbacks of using credit cards, and he shares some helpful and cautionary tips. This book left a big impact on our children.

Professor in a Box: Financial Accounting by Michael P. Licata

This college level course was accessible through CD-ROM delivery. We found this program to be a very thorough and detailed accounting course.

Science

Science in a Nutshell Kits by Delta Education
These are appropriate for the elementary level. We greatly enjoyed many of these hands-on activity kits, which are arranged by topic. They are fun and easy to use. Special materials are included in the kits and lists of everyday supplies needed are provided so you can plan ahead.

Christian Liberty Nature Readers by Christian Liberty Press
This set of readers covers different reading levels. Each text contains interesting descriptions and illustrations of plants and animals. Our children, who love the outdoors, greatly enjoyed reading these books and learning about God's creation.

Apologia elementary school level textbooks, published by Fulbright
As far as elementary aged textbooks go, these are good. I found the explanations to be clear, the activities were interesting, and the illustrations were engaging. Activity companion books are also available.

Apologia high school level textbooks by Dr. Jay L. Wile and other authors
Book topics include (but are not limited to) biology, chemistry, physics, and anatomy. All of the high school level books are extremely thorough and offer great preparation for college level work.

Real Science-4-Kids: Chemistry by Rebecca Keller
This text provides an excellent introduction to chemistry for elementary level students. We had so much fun making our own litmus paper by boiling red cabbage. We also loved making molecules out of marshmallows and toothpicks. This course presented an important body of information in a fun, child-friendly format. Other science topics are also available by the same author.

TOPS Learning Systems by Ron Marson
We enjoyed these fun topical activity-based books. We especially enjoyed the *Green Thumbs: Radishes* guide. We planted radish seeds, measured their growth, graphed data about the plants, and observed

how the plants responded to sunlight and darkness. If you're looking to add a hands-on dimension to a particular topic, check out some of these books.

Snap Circuits by Elenco Electronics
Our younger son loved following the step-by-step guide to making electrical circuits. This provided a great hands-on introduction to electricity.

Matter & Motion in God's Universe by A Beka Book
This text is most appropriate for the junior high level student. It clearly explains topics such as: astronomy, matter, fluids, heat, energy, flight, fossils, magnets, and electricity. We found this to be a very interesting textbook.

Music

Music Ace software by Harmonic Vision
This is a fantastic computer CD which teaches note reading, tone, pitch, and more. The animation and games were adorable. Our family is not particularly musically inclined, so this was a great course for us.

Great Christian Hymn Writers by Jane Smith and Betty Carlson
This book is a compilation of short stories explaining the history of famous hymns and their composers. We found this book to be powerful, moving, and memorable.

Home Economics

Home Economics by Christian Light
Our young teenaged daughter greatly enjoyed this workbook series, which covered food preparation, childcare, sewing, and more.

Foreign Language

Rosetta Stone Homeschool by Rosetta Stone
This computer software is available in multiple languages. The program provides interactive and fun activities to help the student learn a foreign

language. The homeschool versions are perfect for recordkeeping and are enjoyable and easy to use.

These are the materials we found most useful and enjoyable. Homeschool materials are continually increasing and improving, so have fun researching and trying new products that are out there. Know your needs, know your likes and dislikes, pray about it, research, and enjoy whatever you choose. Don't let your materials drive you; you are in charge and can adapt them or replace them with others if you desire. Remember, there is no such thing as perfect curriculum. The goal is to raise up godly children who are educated and can think for themselves.

CONCLUSION

I HAVE BEEN PRAYING for you. My heart is to encourage Christian mothers like you and help you believe you *can* successfully homeschool your children. I want you to experience the blessings and fruitfulness we have enjoyed. I want you to realize the incredible rewards that come from investing the time in homeschooling your children and teaching them to seek God's presence. The Bible says, **"He shall receive a blessing from the Lord and righteousness from the God of his salvation. This is the generation of those who seek Him, who seek Your face-even Jacob. Selah" (Psalms 24:5,6).** Let's raise up a generation of those who seek God's face, for they will impact the world for Jesus Christ!

All too soon, your children will grow up and move on. NOW is your time to hold them close, teach them God's ways, love, laugh, and live life together. Homeschooling is not some magic formula; it is not an insurance policy that guarantees your kids will turn out well. Homeschooling is, however, an amazing investment in the lives of your children. It is the parenting path that inarguably provides the maximum amount of time for you to spend with your children, and it enables you to journey through life together.

When your children see real faith walked out and they are nurtured in a loving, safe, and accepting atmosphere, they are more likely to choose to walk in the same manner. When you invest your life in training your children, making them your greatest priority after God and your marriage, you can rest in the knowledge that you will have done your utmost for His highest.

If you have taken the time to read this book, then God has likely placed homeschooling on your heart. Let me encourage you to step out in faith and do it. God will help you along the way. There are no perfect parents; there is no secret homeschool formula. There are simply parents who love God, who love their families, and who want to do their best to train up their children in the Lord. Do not fear making mistakes along the way, for mistakes are part of the learning process.

My prayer is that God will continue to raise up Christian families to shine brightly for His name. Homeschooling provides an unparalleled arena for training. You will never regret spending more time with your children; you will be forever thankful that you did. I know that if God has called you, then He will empower and equip you. Enjoy the blessing; you can do it!

And Jesus said to him, "'If You can?' All things are possible to him who believes" (Mark 9:23).

Arms full of blessings

Siblings

First day of homeschool

Buddies

Fun in the snow

Beginner hunter

Luke and Mom

Dad with kids and piglets

Treats at the fair

Making castles

Matching dresses

Playing pretend

Bottle feeding a calf

The very first egg

Fishing with Dad

Riding horses with Dad

Outdoor fun

Brothers on a fishing trip

A new helmet

Honey sales

Driving the tractor

Learning about engines

Skiing

Snowmobile trip

In the Alps

Ice skating in France

Switzerland

Cheese

New Zealand glacier

New Zealand highlands

Getting water in Nicaragua

Snowmobiling in Yellowstone

Mud wars

Boat ride in the Everglades

Elizabeth and Dad fishing

Husking corn

Checking on cows

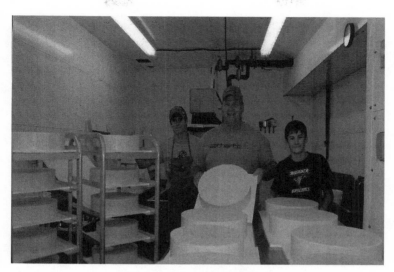

Making cheese with Dad

Luke wrestling

Brother sister quad ride

Showing cattle at the fair

Schoolwork with Mom

Siblings hunting

Aldan's favorite

Family photo

WORKS CITED

Adams-Gordon, Beverly. *Spelling Power.* Pomeroy: Castlemoyle Books, 1997.

Anderson, Jan. *World Literature.* Pensacola: A Beka Book, 2011.

Andreola, Karen. *Story Starters.* Quarryville: Charlotte Mason Research and Supply Co., 2006.

Andrew, Brother. *God's Smuggler.* Minneapolis: Chosen, 2017.

Ankers, Angela. *Step-by-Step Grammar.* Summerbook Company, 2000.

Baker, Sandy. *Writing Doodleloops: Creative Whole Language Activities for Beginning Writers.* Good Apple, 1993.

Bauer, Susan Wise. *The Story of the World: Volume 3: Early Modern Times.* Charles City: Peace Hill Press, 2004.

—. *The Story of the World Activity Book Four: The Modern Age.* The Well-Trained Mind Press, 2005.

—. *The Story of the World: History for the Classical Child: Volume 4: The Modern Age.* Charles City: Peace Hill Press, 2015.

—. *The Story of the World: Volume 4: The Modern Age.* Charles City: Peace Hill Press, 2005.

Berg, Hilary. *History of the Horse.* Sandwich: Beautiful Feet Books, 1997.

Berg, Rea. *A Literature Approach to US and World History.* Sandwich: Beautiful Feet Books, 2010.

—. *Ancient History: A Literature Approach.* Sandwich: Beautiful Feet Books, 1995.

—. *Early American History: A Literature Approach for Primary Grades*. Sandwich: Beautiful Feet Books, 1992.

—. *Literature Approach to Geography*. Sandwich: Beautiful Feet Books, 1994.

Bowen, William, and George Thompson. *American Government in Christian Perspective*. Pensacola: A Beka Book, 2012.

Brady, Esther Wood. *Toliver's Secret*. New York: Dell Yearling, 2000.

Brenneman, Ben. *Simply Writing the Five-Paragraph Essay*. Boxborough: Pathways Publishing, 2004.

Brookes, Mona. *Drawing with Children*. New York: G.P. Putnam, 1996.

Burchers, Sam. *Vocabulary Cartoons II: SAT Word Power*. Punta Gorda: New Monic Books, 2013.

Burkett, Larry, and Ed Strauss and Ken Save. *The World's Easiest Pocket Guide to Getting Your First Credit Card*. Chicago: Northfield Pub., 2000.

Calvert. *Calvert School Interactive Spelling and Vocabulary*. Calvert, 1998. CD.

Cardulla, Frank. *The Great Courses: Chemistry*. The Teaching Company, n.d. DVD.

Chambers, Oswald. *My Utmost for His Highest*. Westwood: Barbour and Company, Inc., 1963.

Chapman, Gary. *The 5 Love Languages of Children*. Chicago: Northfield Pub., 2012.

Cheaney, Janie, and Tielman Cheaney. *Wordsmith Apprentice*. Humansville: DGC, 1995.

Christian Liberty Nature Readers Set. Christian Liberty Press, 1996.

Clarkson, Clay, and Sally Clarkson. *Educating the Wholehearted Child*. Whole Heart Ministries, 2001.

D'Aulaire, Ingri, and Edgar Parin D'Aulaire. *D'Aulaire's Book of Greek Myths*. Doubleday Books for Young Readers, 1962.

Davis, Chris and Ellyn Davis. *I Saw the Angel in the Marble*. Crossville: Elijah Press, 2004.

Davis, Chris. *Turning Hearts*. Elijah Company, 2004. CD.

Demme, Steven. *Stewardship Biblical Foundations*. Math U See, 2009.

—. *Stewardship: A Biblical Approach to Personal Finance*. Math U See, 2009.

DeYoung, Donald B. *Science and the Bible: 30 Scientific Demonstrations Illustrating Scriptural Truths*. Grand Rapids: Baker Books, 1994.

Engelmann, Siegfried. *Teach Your Child to Read in 100 Easy Lessons*. New York: Simon & Schuster, 1986.

Fisher, Richard. *Pre-Algebra Concepts*. Los Gatos: Math Essentials, 2008.

Forbes, Esther Hoskins. *Johnny Tremain*. Boston: Graphia, 2011.

Forster, Pam. *For Instruction in Righteousness: A Topical Reference Guide for Biblical Child-Training*. Gaston: Doorposts, 1995.

Foster, Genevieve. *Abraham Lincoln's World*. New York: Scribner, 1975.

—. *George Washington's World*. New York: Scribner, 1975.

Foster, Ruth, and Michelle Breyer. *A Word a Week Vocabulary Program*. Teacher Created Resources, 1999.

Fulbright, Jeannie. *Exploring Creation with Zoology 1: Flying Creatures of the Fifth Day*. Anderson: Apologia Educational Ministries, 2005.

—. *Exploring Creation with Zoology 3: Land Animals of the Sixth Day*. Anderson: Apologia Educational Ministries, 2006.

Garfield, Leon. *Shakespeare Stories*. Boston: Houghton Mifflin Company, 1985.

Getty,Barbara, and Inga Dubay. *Italic Handwriting Series*. Portland: Continuing Education Press, 1994.

Grocery Cart Math. Melrose: Common Sense Press, 2011.

Hake, Stephen, and John Saxon. *Saxon Math 5/4 Homeschool: Complete Kit 3rd Edition*. Norman: Saxon Publishers, 2004.

—. *Saxon Math Homeschool 6/5*. Norman: Saxon Publishers, 2005.

Hake, Stephen, and John Saxon. *Saxon Math Homeschool 7/6*. Norman: Saxon Publishers, 2004.

Hakim, Joy. *A History of US*. New York: Oxford University Press, 2006.

Hall, Nancy. *Explode the Code 1*. Cambridge: Educators Pub Svc Inc, 1984.

Harnadek, Anita. *Math Word Problems*. Pacific Grove: Critical Thinking Books & Software, 1996.

Henry, Marguerite. *Misty of Chincoteague*. New York: Aladdin, 1947.

Hillyer, V. M. *A Child's History of the World*. Nielsen Bookdata, 2011.

Hindley, Judy. *The Usborne Time Traveler*. Tulsa: EDC Pub., 1999.

Hiskes, Dolores G. *Phonics Pathways: Clear Steps to Easy Reading and Perfect Spelling*. San Francisco: Jossey-Bass, 2005.

Holling, Holling C. *Minn of the Mississippi*. Boston: Houghton Mifflin Company, 1979.

—. *Paddle-to-the-Sea*. Boston: Houghton Mifflin Company, 1969.

—. *Seabird*. Boston: Houghton Mifflin Company, 1975.

—. *Tree in the Trail*. Boston : Houghton Mifflin, 1990.

Home Economics. Harrisonburg: Christian Light Publications, 1980.

Hopkins, Diane. *Happy Phonics*. Love to Learn, Inc., 2007.

Husted, Terri. *Math Detective*. Pacific Grove: Critical Thinking Books & Software, 2003.

Jackson,Dave, and Neta Jackson. *Hero Tales*. Minneapolis: Bethany House Publishers, 1996.

Johnson, Crockett. *Harold and the Purple Crayon*. New York: HarperCollins, 2016.

Keller, Rebecca W. *Real Science 4 Kids: Chemistry Level I*. Albuquerque: Gravitas, 2008.

Kemmerer, Susan. *Apples: Daily Spelling Drills for Secondary Students*. Telford: Schoolhouse Publishing, 2001.

—. *Research in Increments*. Schoolhouse Publishing, 2004.

Kemper, Dave, and Ruth Nathan and Patrick Sebranek. *Write Away: A Handbook for Young Writers and Learners*. Wilmington: Great Source, 2002.

Lambert, Jane. *Five in a Row: Volume I*. Grandview: Five in a Row, 1997.

Lane, Christopher, and Sharon Dahl. *Kingdom Parables*. Wheaton: Victor Books, 1994.

Larson. *Saxon Math 1 Homeschool: Complete Kit 1ˢᵗ Edition*. Norman: Saxon Publishers, 1994.

—. *Saxon Math 2 Homeschool: Complete Kit 1ˢᵗ Edition*. Norman: Saxon Publishers, 1994.

—. *Saxon Math 3 Homeschool: Complete Kit 1ˢᵗ Edition*. Norman: Saxon Publishers, 1994.

Licata, Michael P. *Financial Acccounting*. Professor in a Box LLC, 2018. CD-ROM.

Lifepac Civics. Chandler: Alpha Omega, 2000.

Lundquist, Joegil. *English from the Roots Up*. Bellevue: Literacy Unlimited, 1999.

MacDonald, Betty. *Mrs. Piggle-Wiggle*. New York: HarperCollins, 2007.

Majors, Katie Davis. *Kisses from Katie*. New York: Howard Books, 2012.

Manor, Rebecca. *History of Science Study Guide*. Beautiful Feet Books, n.d.

Marks, Dave. *Writing Strands*. Houston: National Writing Institute, 2007.

Marson, Ron. *Green Thumbs: Radishes*. TOPS Learning Systems, 1998.

Marson, Ron, and Peg Marson. *TOPS Learning Systems: Floating and Sinking*. Canby: TOPS Learning Systems, 1995.

Martin, Mildred. *Missionary Stories with the Millers*. Mifflin: Green Pastures Press, 2009.

Maslen, Bobby Lynn, and John Maslen. *Bob Books*. New York: Scholastic, 2007.

Matter & Motion in God's Universe. Pensacola: A Beka Book, 1994.

Maybury, Richard. *Whatever Happened to Penny Candy?* Placerville: Bluestocking Press, 2015.

McGraw, Eloise Jarvis. *The Golden Goblet*. New York: Puffin Books, 1986.

McHugh, Michael, and John Southworth. *Story of the Middle Ages*. Arlington Heights: Christian Liberty Press, 2002.

Meyer, Joyce. *Battlefield of the Mind*. New York: Faith Words, 1995.

Millard, Anne. *Usborne Book of World History*. London: Usborne, 1985.

Morgan, Teresa. *Days on the Farm with Annette and Samuel*. Crockett: Rod and Staff, 1987.

Music Ace. Chicago: Harmonic Vision, 2004. CD.

Notgrass, Ray. *Exploring World History*. Gainesboro: Notgrass Company, 2014.

Omartian, Stormie. *The Power of a Praying Parent*. Eugene: Harvest House Publishers, 2014.

—. *The Power of a Praying Wife*. Eugene: Harvest House Publishers, 2017.

Osborne, Mary Pope. *Favorite Medieval Tales*. New York: Scholastic Press, 1998.

Pearl, Debi. *Created To Be His Help Meet*. Pleasantville: No Greater Joy Ministries, 2004.

Pearl, Michael. *In Search of a Help Meet*. Pleasantville: No Greater Joy Ministries, 2013.

Phillips, Wanda. *Daily Grams*. Scottsdale: ISHA Enterprises, 2002.

—. *Easy Grammar Plus*. Scottsdale: ISHA Enterprises, 1995.

Plant, Cherie. *Editor in Chief Series*. Seaside: Critical Thinking Co., 2011.

Pudewa, Andrew. *High School Essay Intensive, Second Edition*. Institute for Excellence in Writing, 2017. DVD.

—. *Student Writing Intensive Level A Curriculum*. Locust Grove: Institute for Excellence in Writing, 2010.

Queen, Sandi. *Language Lessons for the Elementary Child*. New Freeport: Queen Homeschool Supplies, 2006.

Quine, David. *Starting Points*. Richardson: Cornerstone Curriculum, 2002.

Rasmussen, Lore, and Robert Hightower and Peter Rasmussen. *Miquon Math Student Book Set*. Key Curriculum Press, 2010.

Rasmussen, Steven. *Key to Decimals*. Berkeley: Key Curriculum Press, 1985.

—. *Key to Percents*. Berkeley: Key Curriculum Press, 1988.

Rasmussen, Steven, and Peter Rasmussen. *Key to Algebra*. Berkeley: Key Curriculum Press, 1975.

Repko, Linda. *Science in a Nutshell: Electrical Connections*. Nashua: Delta Education, 1999.

Retzer, Carol Ann, and Eva Hoshino. *A Reason for Handwriting*. Siloam Springs: Concerned Communications, 2001.

Richardson, Joy. *Looking at Pictures*. Harry N. Abrams, 1997.

Rosetta Stone Homeschool German Level 1. Rosetta Stone, Inc., n.d. DVD.

Rosetta Stone Homeschool Spanish. Rosetta Stone Inc., n.d. DVD.

Sabouri, Greg. *Geometry: A Teaching Textbook*. Teaching Textbooks Inc., 2005.

Saxon, John. *Algebra 1/2: An Incremental Development*. Norman: Saxon Publishers, 1997.

—. *Algebra 2: An Incremental Development, 2nd Edition*. Norman: Saxon Publishers, 1991.

—. *Algebra I: An Incremental Development, 3rd Edition*. Norman: Saxon Publishers, 2003.

Science in a Nutshell: Charge It! Static Electricity. Nashua: Delta Education, 1998.

Science in a Nutshell: Electrical Connections. Nashua: Delta Education, 1999.

Science in a Nutshell: Flight! Gliders to Jets. Nashua: Delta Education, 1999.

Science in a Nutshell: Gears at Work. Nashua: Delta Education, 1999.

Science in a Nutshell: Magnet Magic. Nashua: Delta Education, 1999.

Science in a Nutshell: Rock Origins. Nashua: Delta Education, 1999.

Sebranek, Patrick. *Write Source 2000*. Wilmington: Great Source, 1999.

—. *Writers INC.* Wilmington: Great Source, 2001.

Selsam, Millicent E. *Greg's Microscope.* New York: Harper & Row, 1990.

Sewell, Anna. *Black Beauty.* Racine: Whitman Publishing Company, 1955.

Sillinger, Doug. *Lego Crazy Action Contraptions.* Klutz, 2008.

Simonson, Dr. Leslie. *The WIN Program: Writing in Narrative.* The Elijah Company, 1996.

Smith, Jane Stuart, and Betty Carlson. *Great Christian Hymn Writers.* Wheaton: Crossway Books, 1997.

Snap Circuits. Wheeling: Elenco Electronics, Inc., 2017.

Speare, Elizabeth George. *The Bronze Bow.* New York: Houghton Mifflin Co., 2007.

—. *The Witch of Blackbird Pond.* New York: Yearling Book, 1997.

Ten Boom, Corrie, and Elizabeth and John Sherrill. *The Hiding Place.* Grand Rapids: Chosen Books, 2006.

Tripp, Tedd. *Shepherding a Child's Heart.* Wapwallopen: Shepherd Press, 2005.

Trocki, Phillip. *Spelling Workout Level C Pupil Edition.* Cleveland: Modern Curriculum Press, 1994.

Troxel, Larry, and Kathy Troxel. *Geography Songs.* Newport Beach: Audio Memory, 2010. CD.

Trumbull, H. Clay. *Hints on Child Training.* Great Expectations Book Co., 1993.

Typing Instructor. Pleasanton: Individual Software, Inc., 2000. CD.

Virkler, Mark. *Dialogue with God.* Gainsville: Bridge-Logos, 2005.

Watson, Sharon. *Jump In: A Workbook for Reluctant and Eager Writers.* Anderson: Apologia Educational Ministries, Inc., 2006.

Websters II New Riverside University Dictionary. Boston: Houghton Mifflin, 1984.

Wigglesworth, Smith. *Greater Works*. New Kensington: Whitaker House, 1999.

Wilder, Laura Ingalls. *The Little House (9 Volumes Set)*. New York: Harper Trophy, 1994.

Wile, Jay. *Exploring Creation with Biology*. Apologia Educational Ministries, 2005.

—. *Exploring Creation with Chemistry*. Anderson: Apologia Educational Ministries, 2003.

Wile, Jay, and Marilyn Shannon. *The Human Body: Fearfully and Wonderfully Made*. Anderson: Apologia Educational Ministries, Inc., 2001.

Williams, Jane, and Rick Maybury. *A Bluestocking Guide to Economics*. Placerville: Bluestocking Press, 2010.

Wilmerding, Elsie, and Alexandra Bigelow. *Just Write*. Cambridge: Educators Publishing Service, 2001.

—. *Just Write: Book 3*. Educators Publishing Service, Inc., n.d.

Wilwerding, Walter. *How to Draw and Paint Hoofed Animals*. Tustin: Foster Art, 1987.

Wise Bauer, Susan, and Jessie Wise. *The Well-Trained Mind: A Guide to Classical Education at Home*. New York: W. W. Norton & Company, 2009.

Zaner-Bloser. *Zaner-Bloser Handwriting*. Columbus: Zaner-Bloser, 2012.

Made in the USA
Middletown, DE
27 June 2021